REFLECTIONS OF A BLACK MAN

CURTIS E. CAMPBELL, SR.

Outskirts Press, Inc.
Denver, Colorado

Reflections of a Black Man
All Rights Reserved
Copyright © 2006 Curtis E. Campbell, Sr.

Outskirts Press
http://www.outskirtspress.com

ISBN-10: 1598008307
ISBN-13: 9781598008302

Outskirts Press and the "OP" logo are trademarks belonging to Outskirts Press, Inc.

Printed in the United States of America

REFLECTIONS OF
A
BLACK MAN

DEDICATION

This book is dedicated to the extraordinary women who through their strength and wisdom, taught me forgiveness, patience, and most of all, love.

Thanks to my Great Grandmothers Essie Mae Wright and Janie Campbell, you gave the family continued roots and guided us through the harshest times.

To Grandmas Beatrice Campbell and Beatrice Martin, your patience and wisdom played a vital role in keeping the family together.

To my mother Susan, it was you who had the strength to ensure men were created from little boys.

To my wife Tammy, thank you for being a wonderful wife and an even better mother.

Aunt Sarah, you have always been my light at the end of the tunnel and have always been more of a mother to me than an aunt.

To my aunts, Nell, Janie, Ruby Mae, and Willie Mae, thank you for the continued love and support you have given me throughout the years. You never judged as your love is unwavering and unconditional.

Special thanks to my legacy, Curtis E Campbell, Jr. and my friend for over 20 years Michael R. Hill.

INTRODUCTION

"Reflections of a Black Man" takes you on a journey with an African American boy growing up in the Low Country of South Carolina. Though Chris feels as if he is being pin-balled around the community, there are lessons learned and applied with every decision and move.

The questions are, "which lessons should be implemented into the development of his manhood?" Should some of these lessons be thrown away by the wayside as they serve no purpose to the goals that he is trying to achieve? Chris must make these decisions and ultimately pay the price for them.

"Reflections" will make some cry, some mad, and even make some laugh. As Chris finds out, we cannot always predict our destination or the opportunities that will be presented to us, but we certainly can control and make the best of them. This is a story about Chris and his memories; the great times as well as the bad.

TABLE OF CONTENTS

CHAPTER 1
INNOCENCE

An African-American baby boy is born with innocence, full of energy, and with no idea of what he is about to endure in this world. He knows no prejudice as the first face he sees is the white doctor that delivers him to his mother.

Though his mother is only 15 years old, there is a strong family bond that already links this baby boy to his extended family. This is the 60's, and the extended family relies on each other without the help of government assistance, which doesn't exist. Though the family is very poor monetarily, the child will never know it as everyone pitches in to claim him as their own.

If there was one advantage that the southern poor blacks had over the northern poor blacks, it was the easy access of food from crops, the creek, the forest, and the love from the extended family. In the south, blacks had the fields, livestock, and an abundance of seafood from the creek to fall back on when money was scarce. The fields grew beets, turnip greens, squash, corn, tomatoes, beans, sugarcane, cucumbers, okra, and watermelons. The woods were full of rabbits, squirrels, possums, deer, birds, raccoons, berries, and edible weeds. There was always fish, shrimp, blue crabs, crayfish, conch, and oysters from the creek.

This was the innocence a small black child named Chris was introduced to in a small town called Seabrook in Beaufort, South Carolina. This was a time when money and social status seemed insignificant. My cousins and I would jump up and down just to see a dirt road being paved, another field being cleared for crops, a crab boil, which people now call frogmore stew, being started, or just steaming oysters on an old piece of aluminum outside. We would explore a three-mile radius for hours, knowing what berries and grapes were safe to eat and what weeds could be sucked on for refreshment.

Life was so full of joy as my grandma Baybe would be sitting on the couch knitting a quilt and cooking a stew on the stove. It sometimes took several months for my grandma Baybe to finish one of her quilts, but when it was done, she explained how another chapter in our generation was completed. Much of the quilt that Grandma Baybe made was from old clothing from relatives that had long passed away.

The quilt was a way for us to remember who they were. The quilts were a part of Uncle Knoot, Uncle Robert, Uncle Rufus, Uncle William, Grand Aunt Nussie, and many other relatives who were talked about all of the time. The quilts also played a significant role in letting us know that we were bonded in death as well as life. In many ways, I was blessed to be around her and her wisdom. Just imagine, at that particular time in my life, I had Grandma Baybe, Grandma Bebe, Great Grandma Dadah, and Great Grandma Janie. To have that many grandparents alive at one time was truly amazing. There were absolutely no doctors, lawyers, or scholars who could have taught me more in life than those four extraordinary women.

My mother and I lived with my grandma Baybe, my aunt Julie, and her children. The summers were extra hot because we did not have any air-conditioning, and the winter was extra cold because the tiny 500-foot square board house did not have any insulation. Since there was no indoor plumbing, we would bathe in a big tin tub on the outside in the summer and boil water to add with the cold water in the winter. No one complained and all of us were as happy as children could possibly be. The air was pure and there were no additives or preservatives in the foods we ate.

Grandma Baybe always made sure that we ate until we were absolutely full and could not eat any more. The house had eight people living under one roof, but with the love we shared, the small board house seemed like a mansion. For me, things could not have been better, but like everything in life, it would not stay that way. My parents thought that it would be a good idea for all of us to finally live together as a family, and that is when my fortunes would take a turn for the worse.

At the age of four, things really became horrific for me. My mother, who was only 19 years of age, decided to get married and move in with my father, who definitely was not ready to raise a family. The next year would be the worst life a toddler could experience. As it turned out, my father Shane was an uneducated African-American male who felt slighted by the system and took it out on his family. When he walked in the house, my mother and I were so scared that no one ever said anything. Sometimes he would go away for weeks at a time and I would just be elated. The problems always started once he came back. My mother would question him about his absence and his affairs with other women, which was not good for either one of us.

After he would slap her around for what seemed like an eternity, I would surely be on deck. I witnessed my mother being strangled, punched, kicked, and once my father even tried to drown her in the bathroom toilet. As a child, I did not understand why my mother and I had to accept his abuse, and I must admit, I hated my father more than anyone I had ever met. I would pray to God every night to kill him so the abuse would stop.

My mother attended night school to finish her high school diploma. Many of those times, I was left alone with my father. My job was to watch the clock and make sure he was awake in time to pick up my mother. With that much pressure on a four-year-old, telling the right time can be extremely challenging. If I was early or late for the appointed time, I was beaten with belts, straps, shoes, clothes hangers, and anything that he could find. Today I still wonder how bad a four-year-old could have possibly been to deserve that kind of abuse. Did he not like himself that much and decided to take it out on me? He would even take a drill out to scare me by telling me he was going to put it through my hands. On one particular night, I was chasing a butterfly, as I have always been fascinated by them, and ended up breaking an ashtray during my pursuit. That brutal beating was ultimately the signal for my mother to leave. That night when she came home from night school and took my clothes off for my nightly bath, she looked at me and just started screaming. I had welts all over my body.

She rushed me to the hospital and, amazingly, they gave me some ointment and sent me home. In those days, there was no such thing as child abuse. It took four days before my mother could bathe me adequately because of the amount of scars on my body. It was against the law for a white man to lynch someone of color, so why did my father feel like it was right to lynch me, a product of himself? Black people were taught that the only way a child can be disciplined is through fear and beatings. All of the self-respect and esteem a child has can be beaten right out of them if a parent is not careful.

We packed up and left after that, but each time we had left before, my father Shane would find us and bring us back to the house of horror. My mother did not tell anyone about this, because as I tell my aunts and grandparents about the horrors I went through, they find it absolutely hard to believe. I often ask adults, "Why keep secrets that can scar your children emotionally for life?" Today, my uncle Quinn tells me that my father was just a product of an earlier generation of abuse from his father. He told me that my grandfather treated my father the same way and he just thought that that was the acceptable way of raising a black boy in a tough world. I may be in the minority, but I have always felt that using the excuse of being abused by your parents is a lame excuse when abusing your child. So many African-American males are fatherless, but is it better to be fatherless than to have a father in the household that constantly abuses the family? I am sure that many of my problems, like wetting the bed at age four, fear of a conversation with a male in my youth, and having nightmares were directly associated with the physical and emotional abuse I received from my father. Often when I wanted to sit down and talk to my mother about the abuse, she would get very sad and just say that she did not remember most of it. I question sometimes if she really does not remember most of it, but my wife also tells me that she cannot remember the abuse that she too endured when she was very young. Sometimes, people choose to block out traumatic times in their lives, but amazingly, I can remember every traumatic experience I have ever encountered. My aunt Cynthia has a saying that I will never forget. She would say, "Be careful how you treat kids because one day they will grow up." One day that child will grow up and have a family of his or her own. What will become of him or her when there is nothing to emulate except torture, deception, and infidelity that they witnessed as a youth?

Before my fifth birthday, my mother gave birth to another son. For a moment, things were better and most of the attention was given to my new brother. It seemed as if the beatings stopped overnight. My brother Tom became my best friend, and we were very close. When he started walking, he got into everything. He was very curious and always seemed to have a smile on his face. One day, he and I were playing outside when he turned up missing. At the time, I had just turned five years old and my brother was almost two. Somehow, my brother had wandered off to the local fire station that was next door. Once the fireman brought my brother home and had left, I was given a beating in front of the entire neighborhood as my mother just watched.

I thought I deserved it, but now I know that you should not put that kind of responsibility on any five-year-old, yet alone beat his brains out for it. Needless to say, under today's laws, my parents would have been identified as unfit, and I am sure that I would have been given to the state or another family member. Though my mother did not apply the abuse directly, at the time she did not do enough to ensure the safety of Tom and I. I believe that there is an absolute difference between beating a child and spanking a child, and believe me when I say that I still have the marks to prove that they were beatings. My mother had left my father several times, and it would actually take him a week sometimes to find out that we were even gone. He always knew exactly where to find us as he would roll up in his deuce and a quarter and shuttle us back to hell. If there was one fortunate thing about all of this, it is that my brother never experienced the wrath that I did, but I knew that if he was just a little older, the torture would have been dealt evenly. It is easy to question yourself when you are a child because you think sometimes you deserve to be treated badly.

My mother tried to make up for the abuse by taking me shopping with her. That was always a great experience as she would leave me with the local town barbers and they would take care of me like I was one of their own while she did her shopping. Watching the 6 o'clock news was very unnecessary if you had a chance to go to the local barber shop. You were privy to more than just news, weather, and sports. You also knew who was gay, who cheated on taxes, the local prostitutes, and who went to jail for selling moonshine or bootlegging. The guys sat in the barber shop with their naturals to the ceiling and brim on the hat rack. Everyone was there from pimps, to local hustlers, to legitimate business men. In those days, the barber shop was more than just a place to get a quick haircut, it was an association of men who came together weekly to discuss the signs of the times. It was a place for men to be heard and get their points across when otherwise, they would have been ignored. Everyone was on equal ground and no one was beyond approach. If you were a lawyer, "so what!" If you were an undertaker, "so what!" If you were jobless, homeless, or toothless, "so damn what", you were heard in the barber shop.

My mother would also take me to the local Piggly Wiggly grocery store to buy me a couple of balloons. She knew that I just loved balloons, and for a moment, life was great until we got back to the little white house in downtown Beaufort near Duke Street we called home. My mother was not a lazy woman as she would go to work every day. My father never seemed to quite bring home a full paycheck due to drinking, gambling, and womanizing. This would be a reason to hand out a few ass whippings here and there before dinner. You see, many of the local men would work all week hanging sheet rock. They would indeed make good money but much of it never reached the intended family. Every Friday, a small local store named "Dobbs" was the meeting place for all with a weekly paycheck. A special area was set up for gambling as the men would jeopardize their entire weekly earnings on a game of craps. Some women were smart enough to arrive at Dobbs store before their husbands to get the money for rent and other incidentals, but many women did not take that chance as it was seen as a sign of disrespect by most men in the community. If their husbands came home smiling and upbeat, that meant that he won some money, but if he came home drunk, that meant that he has probably lost most of his weekly earnings and she had better stay clear of him.

During the week, Mom would leave me with a local babysitter near our home. I did not learn anything, but I knew exactly what was going on with the soap operas. When my mother dropped me off and picked me up, my babysitter was the absolute nicest person that I had ever met in the world. In between, I swear she was a bitch. It is funny when you think about it because things would be very good while they were talking and exchanging pleasantries, but once my mother was out of sight, the babysitter had no problem popping us upside the head and screaming profanities. This time however, I knew that I was not the problem because every child in the house was getting it from her. I was smart enough to tell my mother that I was being treated badly by the babysitter, but my she insisted that there was no way that sweet old woman would do such a thing. I still ask myself today, "Why do women, with no patience with their own children, swear up and down that they are capable of babysitting someone else's child?" If your children tell you they are being abused or touched inappropriately by anyone, I encourage you to listen and act or you may ruin an adult before they even have a chance to become one.

CHAPTER 2
MOVING ON

P raise the Lord. Finally my mother got the message and left the brutal dictator I knew as my father. I think she left mostly because she knew she was going to die sooner or later if she did not. My mother's escape to freedom, however, did not come without a price. She decided to move to New York with her uncle and his live-in girlfriend.

Everything happened in a flash as I was only five years old. There was one thing about black folks in the old days, they did not mind giving their children away to relatives. Some of my relatives who grew up thinking that the girl next door was their cousin were in for a rude awakening later in life when they found out that it was actually a sibling. It may have took years, but the cat was always let out of the bag when it came to certain family relations. Most of the time, it happened at the family reunion. The reunions always started innocent enough with family members hugging and kissing, but after a while, and as the day turned into night, stories would start coming out. It seemed like everyone knew once uncle Bill got drunk, he was going to tell it all. As it turned out, it was very surprising to some to find out that the relative they were playing baseball with was their brother, or the girl that they had a crush on for years, was their sister. The older generation simply told some guys not to talk to certain females in the community, but never gave an explanation behind it. Now it was understood, now you knew why they gave the warnings. When I was introduced to my sister Karen, no one had to say a word. It was obvious that she was my sister because of the same facial features. Once it was confirmed that she was my sister, I welcomed her immediately. Some people don't believe in doing that, but what makes my father's blood more pure in me than my half sister? If there is anyone that we should be mad at, it should be the parent, but never the sibling. They did nothing and did not ask to be born. Sometimes you will find that they will actually be a better sibling to you than the ones that you have known all of your life.

As my life became even more complicated, I found myself living with my aunt Cynthia. My mother was gone and my brother was being raised by my great grandmother Dadah. It was hard to understand why my mother chose to leave me with my aunt and my brother with Great Grandmother Dadah when Grandma Baybe was very healthy and still alive. One side of me felt relieved to get away from the brutality of my father, but the other side of me felt alone and uncertain of things to come. How could my mother just leave me? What was happening to my brother? Was my father going to come in the middle of the night and kill me? When my mother ran away before, he would always come to look for us and take us back to the house of hell. At least with my mother, I felt that I had a little bit of protection from the constant ass whippings that he used to dish out. It must have been weeks before I would talk, but when I found out that my father was not going to come and get me, I started to open up a little. My aunt Cynthia had rules in her house, but hers were not accompanied with beatings; instead they were given with explanations. I was a little frightened of her at first, but once I found out the beatings were not going to come, I started to open up to her.

My biggest problem at age five was bed-wetting. I don't know why I did it, but I remember that I would always be dreaming about using the bathroom and before you knew it, I had pissed the bed once more. In those days, babies were not potty-trained, they were trained to potty.

You see, children are not supposed to stop wetting the bed or be potty-trained at the age of two, but the mothers put so much pressure on the children to stop so they would not have to keep buying diapers. Once they thought the children were actually potty-trained, to their dismay, a couple of years later the bed-wetting started over again. This resulted in many kids being five, ten, and even teenagers who still pissed the bed. If you were a pisser, the neighborhood knew because you have to let the mattress air out. If you don't, the entire house will smell like piss. Some parents would put the mattress outside to try to embarrass the child into stopping, but nothing good can come out of putting a mattress with a big piss stain outdoors for the world to see.

My aunt would be furious because she could not afford to just buy another mattress. I shared the bed with my cousin Allen, who was a teenager, and she was not about to put plastic over his mattress. One day, she told me that if I pissed the bed one more time, she was going to tear my bottom to pieces. I did not take that lightly as I had learned to take the threat of receiving a spanking very seriously. The bed-wetting stopped immediately and permanently. My aunt gave me a Mickey Mouse watch to celebrate the occasion. I learned that I could do anything if I was in control of getting it done. Like my mother, my aunt was full of hugs and kisses, but they were not clouded by whippings coming from a man in the house. She was very firm, but she had reasons and explanations behind her actions instead of a belt. She had long discussions with her two children about rights and wrongs instead of trying to correct them with a stick. In those days, our African-American mothers and fathers believed that children should be seen and never heard, especially in public. Also, they believed that children had to have a little fear in them to respect authority. I can understand now why they felt that way. Emmett Till is probably the most popularly known African-American who was lynched and killed by whites in the south, but there were many more who succumbed to the same fate. Your mouth and your eyes could get you killed in the south in the '50s and '60s. That meant that you did not talk back to a white man and you did not gaze at his woman. Doing this could get you killed.

The parents tried to train black kids growing up in the '70s and '80s the same way that they were, but these were different times, and to have an opinion was misconstrued as being ill-mannered. What they actually did was create an afraid, unsure, low self-esteemed and sometimes dejected black man who would not know how to deal with what life was about to dish out. If you are not taught to express yourself as a youth, how would you suddenly get the confidence to do it as an adult? There are various ways to discipline children, which include spankings, but in many ways, the African-American community is just learning how to deal with their children on another level. It was very stereotypical for a black family to use the belt as the only form of discipline. Think back to the television shows that we used to watch and how black parents dealt with their children. On "Good Times," James always referenced the belt as punishment. The same happened to Roger on the television show "What's Happening," but I bet you would not find any reference to a child being spanked on the "Brady Bunch" or the "Partridge Family." "The Cosby Show" was more than just a sitcom for Black America; it was also educational television to show that people of color had culture, good jobs, and could deal with their children both spiritually and intellectually. "The Cosby Show" also taught us that we have the ability to succeed in the corporate world, yet still balance our careers while raising children.

At five, I watched how most of the men would come home beaten from working all day. Their bosses would drop them off in front of their houses, and after taking shit all day, they would decide that they would give their wife a little of it. The men never realized the indignities that their wives or common-law wives encountered also by cleaning someone's house, being a nanny and taking care of someone else's child before she took care of her own, or working in the fields picking crops all day. All the while, she also had to take care of the home and have a meal ready when he got home. Some may disagree, but the black woman had it tougher than any other race that migrated to this melting pot we call the United States. It was she and not the black man who truly kept the household together. It was common for a black man to be married with a family and have a mistress with an entirely different family. No one was exempt from this reality. It was as if there was a critical shortage of black men, so the women in the small neighborhood decided to share the ones who lived there. Though a man may be uncertain, the woman always know that the child is hers, hence the term, "mommas baby, daddy maybe."

That meant that you could be someone's first and second cousin, or be someone's sibling and cousin all at the same time. This type of behavior is taught and prevalent in the Muslim communities like Saudi Arabia and Bahrain, but is not supposed to exist in America. Or, was this our people's way of not totally disregarding their roots back in Africa when men were known to have as many wives as they could support?

I would see my younger brother often, as he lived in a totally different situation than I lived in. He lived with my great grandmother, who had taken in all children that other relatives did not want. My great grandmother Dadah was the eldest person in the family, and if there was turmoil, her word was the last word. People could be arguing about anything under the sun, but when she said enough, that meant that it was over. You could count on seeing everyone from different generations of the family during the week because at one time or another, they were going to Great Grandma Dadah's house to pay their respects. I had never seen my Great Grandfather due to the fact that he had died in the second world war. I was told that he was a great man. Every Independence day until she died, Dadah would have us raise the flag in memory of our Great Grandfather Freddie Wright. We would raise the flag high and we made absolutely sure not to let it ever touch the ground. When my brother and I would see each other, we would play and gravitate toward each other for the moments that we would have, but it seemed as if the time would pass quickly when I was with him. It had to be a great shock to him at two years old to be left with relatives and not know exactly what had happened to his family. My great grandma was a terrific person, but by that time, she was over 70 years of age.

As time went on, my aunt slowly began to give me the confidence that I had been lacking by talking to me and reassuring me that I was special. She must have known that it was a very traumatic time for me and did her best to make me feel a part of the family. I remember getting a visit from my mother on some occasions. She would send money, clothes, and letters to my aunt while she was living in New York. Most of the time, she would visit at night when I was sleeping, but she always woke me up to talk to me. She would not stay long for fear that my father would find out that she was in town and come to get her. I would spend some weekends at my father's parents' house and every time I went there, it was like Christmas.

My grandmother Bebe was the nicest woman that I have ever met in the world. My grandfather had a farm with many animals, and my brother and I would be together for an entire weekend. I can remember nothing but great times at my grandmother Bebe's house. I often tell folks that I had two fantastic grandmothers who were very different. My grandmother Bebe would often make me up a batch of homemade cookies with some milk, while my other grandmother Baybe would send me off to the bootleggers to fetch her a half pint of whiskey. Both were very different and wonderful to me. Grandma Bebe made the best grits, served with homemade bread, country bacon, eggs from the chicken coup, and sausages. For the entire weekend, we would go shopping, eat anything we wanted, and run around the farm until we were dead tired. I think she realized that my father was the scum of the earth, so she tried hard to compensate for his lack of parenting. Most people in town thought that my grandfather was insane as well. I have always been told that my father got all of his traits from my grandfather. Though that may be true, my grandfather never laid a hand on me and always praised me for being a wonderful grandson. He was very well respected within the community and I have to believe that was the case because he was a hard worker and he had a reputation for being trigger happy. That simply means that he did not mind putting a bullet in your ass if you pissed him off. By the time the weekend was over and my grandmother had to take us back, I would be looking at the clock, knowing that my brother and I would be separated once more. I would arrive back at my aunt's about five pounds heavier with new clothes and a pocket full of money. My aunt always made sure that any money intended for my use would be spent on me. As the fifth year of my life passed by, I started getting curious and would ask my aunt about 50 questions a day. She would answer them all without ever showing as little as a frown. One summer, I got ringworm in my head from playing in the fields and not washing my head adequately and my brother had a bad burn on his body from leaning against my great grandmother's iron stove.

My great grandmother's iron stove was used to heat the house, cook dinner, roast potatoes, and bake bread. It was truly amazing what could be done with that stove; however, if you were foolish enough to get too close to that stove, you were going to lose some flesh and bodily fluids. If you were burnt in those days, the old people would try to sooth it by apply butter to it. As we know now, that was some dumb shit but most of the time they got it right. They could not afford to buy medicines, so they concocted medicines from plants and spirits. When my mother returned and saw the condition of my brother, she made a decision to leave New York to be with us.

CHAPTER 3
DYSFUNCTIONAL FAMILY

Once my mother returned from New York, my aunt had a long talk with me. I was in no mood to go back to what I remembered as the most traumatic period of my short life. I was in no mood to be beaten by my father and not know the reason. I was in no mood to see my father abuse my mother or knock another tooth out of her mouth. I remembered whining for all it was worth, but to no avail; the decision already was made that I was indeed going back to my mother and it was final. Obviously I would not have had any issues with going back to my mother as long as my father was absent in the picture. On a positive note, this would give me a chance to be with Tom everyday. To my delight, my mother did not reconcile immediately with my father as we moved in with Grandma Baybe. Unlike my grandma Bebe, Grandma Baybe loved her privacy and lived alone. She loved her family, but she did not like for anyone to have an extended stay. There were only two bedrooms in the house. My brother and I shared a sofa bed while my mother and grandma each had their own rooms. It did not seem like a bad arrangement at first, but after about a month, things started to go south. My mother and grandma would argue all night about things that were very insignificant. You see, Grandma was big on water conservation since that was the only house she had ever owned with running water. When my brother and I would take a bath, the water had to be shut off once it covered our big toe. You could set a timer on it. After about 15 seconds of running the water, you would hear, "Turn that Goddamn water off!" It is very easy to understand why grandma Baybe felt that way. She grew up washing in a foot tub. Basically, the water mostly covered your ankles after you put your feet in the bucket. They were able to wash their entire body that way. If you think about it, there is something that seems very unsanitary about that. My mother would be so frustrated, she would close the door and continue to run the water anyway. They were absolutely best friends when they were not together.

My mother and grandmother also argued about washing the clothes. My grandma thought that we should save water by washing all of the clothes together, but my mother always had at least two separate loads to wash. Other subjects that were contested on a daily basis were the cooking of food, the rearing of the kids, and the cleaning of the house. My grandmother made sure that my mother knew that if she did not approve of her rules, she was free to go. I often felt sorry for my mother and would tell her that it would be alright. A young woman who was only 22 at the time should not have had to go through what she was going through. My mother would often leave my brother and me with our grandmother when she went out. That was the time when my grandmother would start binge drinking. She could consume a couple of half pints of whiskey in no time at all. You would know when she had had enough because that is when she would try to cook or just start crying. The stove would start, and as soon as the pot started boiling, she would be fast asleep. I never quite figured out what grandma Baybe use to put in the pot or what she was trying to cook when she was drinking. When she was sober, she could cook with the best of them, but when she was drinking, I stayed clear of her pot.

I was smart enough to turn off the stove once I saw that my grandma was not going to wake up. Sometimes, though, I was too late, as smoke would engulf the small house.

Somehow my mother had talked my grandmother into letting my father come to stay with us. I immediately started to have nightmares as I was afraid to go near him. I was not yet two years removed from the physical abuse I had taken from this man, and my mother invited him back into the family. My grandmother constantly told my mother that my father was the worst excuse for a man that she had ever seen in her life. Her exact words were, "If that no-good man that you have is a good husband, that billy goat outside will make me one."

That statement was very profound as I believed it as well. After my father returned, it was very surprising not to get any beatings from him. One would wonder why I characterized his punishments as beatings versus spankings, but believe me when I say that they were not spankings. They were harsh, backbreaking, sometimes unconscious ass whippings. The real

REFLECTIONS OF A BLACK MAN • 15

reason the beating discontinued was because of my grandmother. My grandmother Baybe was all of about 90 pounds, but she was a hell-raiser. My father knew that if he had put a finger on any one of us, he may as well have killed us because my grandmother would not have hesitated to pour hot water on him or make a dash for the butcher's knife. On the surface, Shane appeared to be a changed man, but how could he be? He never received counseling of any kind. Even as a young child, I was sure to not be in a position to be alone with him. One mistake was made on a cool fall day.

As Tom and I played with my cousins about a half mile away from home and with my grandmother working at the local packing shed a few miles away, my father and mother ended up being home alone. By the grace of God, my grandmother came back home just in the nick of time as my father was suffocating my mother. He was actually trying to kill her with a pillow as my grandmother was walking in the house. As my grandma reached for the knife, my father escaped, but my mother was already unconscious. I can remember this like it was yesterday.

The paramedics soon came and so did family members. I remember them calling my mother's name and asking her questions that she could not answer. Everyone in the neighborhood was there and I was sure Shane would be no where to be found. Men in the country protect their women relatives to no end as a manhunt was conducted to find him. Men who usually abuse women are cowards and would never stand up to other men. My mother had amnesia for a few days before she finally came to her senses. I have always been somewhat perplexed with why some women feel that they deserve nothing more than to be abused by a man and why they would keep making excuses to protect a man that is abusive in the household. Woman do not deserve to be abused in any way, shape, or form. I tell young men today to seek counseling if they feel that they will abuse their spouse physically or emotionally.

Some women self-esteem is so low, they think that a piece of man is better than no man at all. This behavior is taught, not learned. I think that a woman more or less tries to emulate the mother that she already has in most cases, and when that example is not positive, she tends to incorporate that kind of behavior in her relationship.

My mother told me that my aunt would complain about her relationship with her boyfriend to my great grandmother Dadah and she would say, "You mean to tell me that you want one man all to yourself?" As it turned out, generations carried this same pattern of thinking, thus never having one man that they could truly call their own. This ultimately resulted in fatherless children. This is not to say that they are bad mothers. On the contrary, they are loving mothers, but I will tell you that they just don't get it when it comes to men. They don't get the fact that when you start bringing multiple men around your little girls, your little girls someday will become women who will do the same things that they saw you doing.

As my mother regained her strength and started to get herself together, that was the last time that we all lived together with my father as a family. My mother, brother, and I stayed with my grandmother in a small green block house, but it was far from a home. Grandma and my mother continued to argue every day and night about everything. As I said before, my grandmother loved her whiskey, quiet time, and privacy. With three other people in a house, which was approximately 500 square feet, all of that was gone. It did not matter what part of the house you ended up in, someone was always in your face. I loved both of them to death and really did not know which side I should be on. In many ways, I felt like a detached kid who really did not belong because I knew it was only a matter of time before we would have to pack our bags again.

This was my grandmother's youngest living child. I often wondered why she would treat her like that, knowing that my mother did not have much of a choice but to stay in the situation that she was already in. Maybe my grandma Baybe treated her like that because she got pregnant at the age of 14. Maybe she treated her like that because she married my father against her will. My grandmother Baybe had five children. The youngest, whose name was Bo, drowned in the neighborhood creek as many of the young black men in small southern towns did back then by accident or so called accidents. I do have a vague memory of him, as my mother looks like him with a wig. I remember my grandmother starting to drink heavily at the time of his drowning. As my mother's other siblings would come over, they all would complain about how much my grandmother was drinking and what it was doing to her health. There were no Dr. Phils or television shows with a psychiatrist to tell us that just maybe my grandmother was suffering from depression because her youngest child had died suddenly without warning. I can remember that every time when my grandmother was in a drunken stupor, she would be calling out her son's name all night. I would just lie there on the bed listening but not wise enough to respond. To make matters worse, my grandmother's sister was the bootlegger who sold her the whiskey. Now, that kind of love is very difficult to understand, or did her sister understand what true love really was? It reminds me of a phrase that black folks have been saying for years. "If you have crabs in a pot and one of them is trying to get out, another crab will grab it by the leg and pull it back down to ensure it is given the same fate as the others." My grandma probably was not trying very hard to get out of that pot, but her sister Barbara was not doing anything to help her. What made the situation worse was the fact that social security was only about 300 dollars a month, and Grandma would waste half of that on booze. It also makes you wonder if her sister could have actually known what she was doing to her. You could argue it both ways, but I don't think that I could ever feed into a sibling's addiction without trying to help them.

CHAPTER 4
BOLD MOVE

The time came when my mother had finally had enough of my grandmother's bickering. She had saved up her money, and at the very young age of 23, she decided that she would give it a go on her own. In 1972, that was a very bold move, as she had never been on her own without the assistance of someone else. Though we were still going to have the comfort of being surrounded by family, this was a tremendous step for all of us. We moved about two miles away from my grandmother's house on property owned by the family. Most in the immediate family lived on the land called "heirs'" property. Heirs' property is land that has been passed down from previous generations to the immediate family. No one person in the family owned the land, and if you wanted to stake out a small portion of it to put a mobile home on, you were more than welcome to do so. The local government prevented anyone from putting permanent houses on heirs' property because sooner or later, it felt like it could somehow find a loophole in the system to confiscate the land. If a permanent building was allowed to be built on the property, that would have made the procurement of the land more difficult. Heirs' property is usually prime property that is not too close to the busy freeways near creeks or ponds. See, in the old days of slavery, white slave owners usually had the property closer to town and gave the slaves the property farther back near the water. Later, whites realized their mistakes and sought ways to procure this prime real estate. It was not that easy to get the property back, as freed slaves were given the land for little or nothing as long as the previous white owners could make a profit from crops grown on the land. Once this land was given, freed slaves would just pass the property down to their children, who would then do the same. So, in the Carolinas and many other southeastern states, you have millions of acres of land called heirs' property. The problem with having heirs' property never showed it's ugly side until it was time to pay the taxes on it. No one wanted any part of heirs' property during that time. They did not understand that by not paying the small taxes on the land, the local government would put it up for auction. My aunt Rita always had the dubious task of collecting the money from the family members who lived on it. Though the amount was not much, people still found reasons to bitch, not realizing the repercussions of not paying it. In reality, the older generation will not be around forever and to leave that responsibility on the younger generation will be futile at best.

My mother bought a modest two-bedroom mobile home that she, my brother, and I stayed in. I was now six years old and about to enter the first year of school. Grandma Baybe seemed heartbroken when my mother left and often complained that she had no idea why my mother had moved out of her house. Did she ever think that maybe it was because she told my mother to get the hell out almost every day and night? I was very proud of my mother for taking the necessary steps to raise my brother and me, but I knew that it was still going to be a struggle to keep our family happily together. There was nothing in the past that assured me that it was going to be smooth sailing from here on out. My mother was still in her early 20s and had probably lived the life of a 40-year-old by now. She was known as one of the most beautiful women in town. My father was a very handsome man, but certainly an asshole. Sometimes, we should look less into the outer beauty of someone and look more for substance instead. One would hope that this time around, she would be more selective in the man she chose to be a mate. The fact of the matter was, she could have any man she wanted. When I was with her, I would watch men just stare at her as if she was a movie star.

As I entered the first grade, I was put in a situation with other kids who behaved absolutely terribly. Segregation had longed passed, but you could not tell by the way that the classes were set up. I remember asking my mother why all of the kids in my class were black, but since my parents and most of my relatives were used to having all blacks in the same class, they did not see anything wrong with that. School was terrible, as every day most of us were shuttled off to the principal's office whether we were guilty or not. I actually witnessed little black boys raping little black girls while the teacher was out. Fights often broke out in the classroom, and I was afraid to go to school. After about two months of this, the principal decided that he was just going to beat the hell out of all of the students in that classroom, including me. The principal's name was Mr. Ford, how could I ever forget. To a small kid, Mr. Ford's paddle must have looked huge. What I can remember most about his spankings is that he would stay on one side of your ass. He was definitely a black kid's ass-spanking specialist. It was law in those days that the principal was allowed to spank all kids in the schools, but I swear I never saw one white kid in the office receiving a spanking from the principal.

Some would say that they have had worse and the spanking should not have been a big deal, but I say that it is a very big deal when you have been previously abused by a parent for the first five years of your life. I missed many days from school that year. Some days were missed for being sick and some days were missed for pretending to be sick. Either way, I did not want to go to school knowing that my chances for getting the one-sided ass special were exceedingly good. I also did not want to go through the daily regimen in the classroom, knowing that the teacher did not have any control of six year old students. We had 26 students in that classroom and we had 26 failures. I ask you, how can 26 out of 26 students not pass the first grade? In hindsight, the teacher should have found another occupation and the principal should have been fired, but where were the parents?

How could all of the students not have the ability to move forward to the second grade? I know that I did not stay behind because of my inability to learn because I was reading at the age of four. I was so terrified at four years old, I turned to books for comfort from my father.

My mother would buy me books, and I also received some of them by mail. Reading them always made me feel as if I was part of another world far away from where I was. They made me feel as if I was amongst the stars very far away. With books, you can be anywhere or anyone you want to be. My mother would always sit down and read my new books with me. It did not take long before I learned the words to all of my books. In retrospect, how hard could the first grade have been if I already knew how to read? That was a very long summer after I failed the first grade. As innocent as they appear to be, kids can also be very cruel. The ones in the neighborhood made it very clear to me that I had failed the first grade and that I was a hopeless dumb ass with no future. If for some reason I got the best of them by playing sports, cards, or just name calling, they could always go to the ace in the hole by saying, "You flunked the fucking first grade!" What was puzzling to me is that I was smarter than most of them and somehow they had managed to pass their grades. As I think back, I was the only six-year-old on heirs' property. Most of my older cousins who beat the shit out of me daily were older than I was. To make matters worse, I took after my grandmother with very dark skin. In the '70s, having very dark skin was not viewed in a very positive way. As the saying goes, if you were white, you were right. If you were brown, you could hang around, but if you were black, you had to stay the hell back. My relatives made sure I knew I was as black as the ace of spade.

My mother was a fair-skinned woman, and some of my cousins were mocha in complexion with some even having gray, light brown, or even green eyes. Certainly, the men had to be confused as to why some of them and their wives were my color, yet their children were of all shades with these different colored eyes. I can now understand why some of them must have been frustrated. To work all day for minimum wage to take care of someone else's kid that your wife or common-law wife has put on you is a burden that is hard for any man to digest. When my brother was born, my mother told me that my grandfather took one look at him and told my father that there was no way in hell that that was his son. As it is, my grandfather, father, uncles, and myself are about 5 feet 11 inches at a modest 210 to 220 pounds. My brother that was born after me is about 6 feet 4 inches and 260 pounds. From what I was told, that was a rift in the family from day one. In those days, there were no paternity tests to speak of for the poor, so you either had to accept the child as your own, or torment yourself worrying about it. I have asked my mother if my younger brother and I indeed have the same father and she said yes. I believe her, as I have never known her to tell a lie.

There are many secrets in the family that have been taken to graves. No one is exempt from infidelity, may it be Bill Clinton, Strom Thurman, or Jesse Jackson. People sometimes put too much stock in a person, only to be disappointed. That is why I am never ever surprised when I hear of someone being unfaithful. Yes, he may be a preacher, teacher, CEO, or highly ranked officer, but they all have one thing in common. They all are men and as I have said before, don't ever say what a man won't do because we are capable of doing anything.

Nothing surprises me about people because we all are subject to sins. Show me a man without skeletons and I will show you a dead one. As it is, the secrets that happen in the dark will come to light. A wise man once said, "Three can keep a secret, provided two of them are dead."

It is funny now to think of me being offended because my cousins called me black. Again, it was taught in the south that having dark skin was bad, and if you were of fair skin, you were of more worth than your darker relative. This theory goes back hundreds of years when the darker slaves worked in the fields while the light-skinned slaves with the straighter hair worked in the house. That theory still carries true today as fair-skinned African Americans are given many more opportunities than their darker counterparts. Beauty is thought to be white, while black is most often given a negative status. A child is trained immediately by society of this fact. A white Christmas, snow white, or white Christ are just a few things children are taught to be beautiful. We also learn of the black plague, blacklist, black Sunday, and blackball, so why would a child think that a black face would not be negative? Society put window dressing on this fact in the corporate world by creating what we know as, "Affirmative Action". Though this law put a Band-Aid on the current hiring practices, the networking of the good old boy system has still stood the test of times. To my mother's credit, she managed to always make me feel special and to be proud of my complexion. All in all, I did manage to get through my first four years of elementary school wise beyond my years. I found that grades one through three did come relatively easy once I was put in a better atmosphere that was more conducive to learning. In hindsight, being left behind in the first grade was a blessing instead of a curse because it gave me an opportunity to be a leader.

CHAPTER 5
CONFIDENCE

Middle school was a little more challenging, but I soon found my niche around my peers as I finally felt that I, too, belonged and was just as smart as all of the other children. One day, a group of salesmen came to the school with several instruments in hand. Once I saw the saxophone, I just knew I had to have it. That night, I asked my mother if she could buy it for me, but she stated that she just couldn't afford it. A few years earlier, my mother had bought me an organ.

She always envisioned me playing in the church, and after a year, I was a pretty good organ player. Though I played the organ on the weekends, my heart was really never into it. Once I saw the saxophone, it was instant love. All of the cool cats like Maceo Parker played the saxophone, but the only people I saw playing the organ was old church people or folks on the Lawrence Welk show. Somehow, my mother got in touch with my father and convinced him to take me to the school to get the saxophone. I had not seen my father in years and really did not want to go anywhere with him out of fear. My mother convinced me that it would be alright, and he came by to get me one late afternoon. We did not talk much, as I was still nervous around him. If he was going to buy me the saxophone, I could forget the other things that he had done to me in the past. That night, I took the saxophone home and in no time I was reading and playing music. At that time, life was great, as I felt like I did not have a worry in the world. Some people say, "If it seems too good to be true, then maybe it is." After a few months had passed and I was ahead of my music class, I received a visit from one of the salesmen at school. I recognized him in his plaid pants and Buster Brown shoes a mile away. He whispered something to my band director, and before I knew it, I was in the principal's office with my saxophone to turn into the salesman. As it turned out, my father made the initial payment, but he never made another payment on the saxophone. I was sent back to the classroom full of tears as I wondered why life had dealt me such a bad hand. The embarrassment never occurred to me as I was shell-shocked to say the least. Again, my saxophone was a daily getaway to wherever I wanted to be and now it was gone. The scars I received from the beatings that my father gave me in the past would heal, but this was a scar that I was not certain would go away. This scar was heartfelt, deep, and strong. This scar would be the final impression of the man I knew he was. Not only was I going to miss the music, but our band director, Mr. Earl Douglas, was the only black man I had ever met who had integrity and a sincere interest in my development. He met my father the night I got the saxophone and was close to me from that point on. I guess after speaking with my father, he was convinced that I needed help. I did not go to school the following day because I was too embarrassed. To my surprise, Mr. Douglas called my mother and told her that he had an extra saxophone that he was not using, and if I still wanted to play music, I could use it until she could afford to buy me one. I was in band class the next day with Mr. Douglas' saxophone and a new appreciation for music. Life teaches us all valuable lessons. Mr. Douglas taught me that even in the darkest of times, there is light. He taught me that a little effort can go a long way to meaning the world to someone else. He taught me that men of color could be classy and as articulate as their white counterparts.

Finally, Mr. Douglas taught me what the definition of a man really was. Still today, if I have a little extra, I will give it to someone who is truly in need. Mr. Earl Douglas died the year after I finished middle school, but for the short three years that I knew him, he was a better man in death than most men I have known my entire life. He was and still is one of my hero's and will always be remembered.

For a young black man growing up in the South, life can sometimes be a bit of a struggle. You try to fit in with all of the bad asses, but at the same time, you know deep in your heart that you do not want to head down the same paths as they were going. By the time

I reached the seventh grade, you could almost point out the black kids in the school that you knew were not going to amount to anything. I mean, it was just something about them. They showed no manners to the teachers, they would come to school maybe twice a week, and no one ever went looking for them. In a way, I do hold some of the teachers at fault as well as the parents. Most of the teachers were elated when the troublemakers did not come to school, and you could see it in their faces. I also thought that some of the teachers bunched all of us together and thought that most of us were not going to amount to anything. In the seventh grade, I saw many young black men dropping out of school altogether. It's not that they were stupid or anything, but no one was there to encourage them to stick it out. If they were able to get a full-time job to help out in the home, they were considered successful.

Unfortunately, the parents of these kids chose to ignore the long-term results of this kind of irresponsible decision. That was certainly not an option for me as I wondered why a parent would allow a young 13-year-old child to drop out of school when they had firsthand experience of how harsh the real world was without the ability to read, write, and hone the basic skills necessary for success in this world. Of course it was illegal to hire anyone under 16 years of age to work a full-time job. The employer got away with that by paying them under the table. I will address paying someone under the table in a later chapter for those who do not know what that is. If you are a young 13-year-old kid and fail to deal with the small nuances put before you at that age, more than likely, you are not going to be successful at dealing with major issues as an adult, the equation being prison or death. I still believe, though, that a 13-year-old is incapable of making the decision to drop out of school on his own and the parents must take ownership of that decision. Success in the neighborhood was measured by owning a mobile home and having a few hundred dollars in your pocket by the end of the week. There was not one person who talked to you about the stock market or other investments, and they failed to realize that living from paycheck to paycheck is just another word for being poor.

I remember even having a couple of relatives who decided that school was not what they needed even after they had made it all the way to the 12th grade. The records speak for themselves. I will challenge anyone to visit their local jails and see who makes up most of the population. You will find that the jails are comprised mostly of uneducated African-American men who are fatherless, have low self-esteem, and even some who embrace the idea that three hot meals and a cot is a good deal. Many African-Americans are locked up for child support, petty theft, possession of illegal drugs with the intent to distribute, writing bad checks, or illegal possession of a firearm. My mother would preach to me that I could be anything that I wanted to be, but also stressed that it took no effort on my part to be nothing. She would preach to me that I could be the President of the United States or that bum on the side of the street begging for a dollar, but the option was mine and mine alone. She would further state that nothing in my life would be given to me and everything I would have would require hard work.

When I was a kid, many of the older men in my day believed that it was better for a young man to go to work full-time because that is the way they were raised. A premium was never put on education. After all, weren't you just going to school to get a job anyway? I never saw it that way. Shit, they had a job, I wanted more than just any employment. All of the men in my family were carpenters of sorts. I respected their abilities to build, measure, and construct, but I wanted just a little more than that and knew that I would never drop out of school. It was always a struggle in most of the African-American homes, and another paycheck coming in seemed like the right recipe to escape poverty. My mother would stress getting a part-time job, but I figured that we were already poor and with me working for minimum wage, we were still going to be poor. I wanted to do something most of the men were not doing, I wanted to graduate from high school. Though it seems like a small feat today, graduating from high school was a major accomplishment in the '70s and '80s. Working may have been a quick fix to help out with some finances, but what they could not see or failed to see is that the young generation of men were going to have families of their own one day, and without proper education, the cycle of poverty, womanizing, and being uneducated would repeat itself over and over again.

The year was 1980, and being somewhat mature, I was going to my first prom. Of course, I was nervous as hell because the female I was going to the prom with was older than I was and certainly more experienced when it came to relationships. I was not alone, as my cousin came from New York to go to my school. He was much more advanced than I was. He knew how to dance, how to talk to women, and on top of that, he was a pretty good basketball player.

It seemed at the time that he had it all. He and I would be going to the prom with two friends. An older cousin of ours would drop us off. With all of the talks about girls and what we had done to them, I was still a virgin. Surely at 14, most of the boys in my school and the ones that I hung out with had already had sex with a girl before, at least that is what they were saying, but I had a secret that no one would ever find out. I was a virgin and really hoped that the pressure would not be put on me that night to perform. I was so naïve and sexually uneducated that only a year or so earlier, I believed that babies came out of a woman's butt instead of her vagina. I am sure that I was not the only one whose reputation for being with a girl was on the line, but no one was going to tell. Theresa, who had a crush on me since the second grade was the only girl I had ever kissed to date besides my mother. I would have been comfortable going to the prom with her because I knew that she was not going to put out and I was not going to be pressured to prove my so called manhood. I had to face the music, it was not going to be Theresa and I had to have the courage to deal with someone older and much more experienced than I was. My prom date was Yvette. She was voluptuous for her age and seemed very sure of herself. Her breast was as big as any woman I had ever seen and she was not petite by any stretch of the imagination. In fact, she was a pretty girl but I never asked her to be my girlfriend. Yvette told me that I was going to be her boyfriend. I was wearing a very nice suit I had borrowed from my cousin Ike while her gown was more or less lavender in color. Yvette was the first girl that I had ever danced with slowly. The song was "Don't Say Goodnight" by the Isley Brothers. As we danced to the music, I was starting to sweat profusely as I knew I could be challenged to have sex. I certainly was not ready for that, but for a guy to say no, or to be afraid was considered to be a trait of women, not men. I was taught to think like that from the older men in the family, but like most things that they were teaching me during that time, this too was bullshit. One of my cousins even gave me a condom that he must have had for five years to commemorate the occasion. I did not have the nerve to tell him that I did not even know how a condom felt, yet alone how to actually put one on. Also, I did not have enough confidence in my manhood to actually show it to a female. What if I took it out and the condom was too big for what I was packing? The men always bragged on their manhood of being ten, eleven, or even twelve inches, but that was not the case for me. I knew I was not hung like that because I took out a ruler and in the 7th grade, 7 ¾ inches was all I was packing. Luckily for me, no one was old enough to have a car or go to a hotel, so I was spared that night. We took our pictures, danced a little more, and then said our good-byes with a kiss. My first prom was a success and I handled it great.

CHAPTER 6
ROBERT SMALLS

By this time, I was full of confidence and was pretty popular in school. I was not afraid to approach girls, and you would have never figured out that I was still a virgin by the way I acted; plus, I was pretty athletic to boot.

That year, I met some interesting people, and I was sure I was going to get more than an eighth grade education by the time I left Robert Smalls Middle School. The girls seemed as if they had sprung melons on their chest during the summer and some of the boys were sporting full beards. Of course, some of the boys were sporting full beards because they had probably repeated the eighth grade a couple of times. I knew that some of the kids who were driving to school could not have possibly been 14 or 15 years old. As confident as I thought I was, there were always some bullies who were ready to test the newcomers. In particular, there the school's main bully, whose name was Bubba. Bubba was big on reputation but small on action. He had to be about 18 in the ninth grade, and he scared the hell out of the small kids. It was very clear that even though I was new at this school, I was not going to put up with a school bully's shit. All of my life, I would rather take the ass whipping from a bully one time rather than put up with it for an entire year. Once Bubba found out that he would have to back up what he was saying to me, he left me alone and I never had another problem with him. A bully can only assume that title if you allow it, but if you fight back a little, they will never bother you again because there is always a chance that they will lose. If you lose, it is expected, but if he loses, his entire status as a bad ass is diminished. A couple of guys from my side of town were already in the ninth grade at Robert Smalls Middle School and they knew their way around. They made it a point to look out for me. Bubba's future was cemented in stone. I mean, you just knew it. You knew that something was missing in this young man's life to make him such a miserable person. Not only was he disrespectful to his peers, he was also disrespectful to all adults, be it teachers or bus drivers. Today, he has a lifetime sentence in prison for murder. I sometimes ask myself if people like that could of been saved. I was fortunate enough to get away from my abusive situation which turned my life around, but there are many Bubba's who don't have that chance. They are subjected to abuse in the family until they become young men and are able to make it on their own. Unfortunately, though you escape the abuse in the household, by that time, it is much too late.

The school system in Beaufort County was very strange, as the middle school continued with the eighth and ninth grades. You had to go to another school altogether for grades ten through twelve. As a result of this, the ninth graders were seen as top dogs whereas in any other school system, they would have been seen as chicken shit freshmen. Two guys from my side of town named Trevor and Randy made sure that I was in with the cool crowd. Randy was laid back and on the smooth side, but Trevor, whose nickname was "Truck," was as raw as they came. He was given the nickname "Truck" because his head was twice as long as Sammy Davis Jr's, and as wide as a tractor trailer. The old folks used to say that if a child has a deformed head, it means that the parent did not mold the head when the baby was born. By the looks of Trevor's head, he had to have been dropped a couple of times at birth. Truck, Randy, and I formed a little group called the three amigos. They introduced me to some of the girls in the ninth grade, and it seemed like one of them always had access to an automobile. I was the only one without a father in the home, and I knew that my mother was not going to let me drive around in her car, especially since I did not have a driver's license. If we could not get to the places that we wanted to, Trevor's older sister Esther would take us. He could always recruit her to take us to places that older adults would have absolutely refused to take us to. Often when we wanted to see a rated "R" movie or a flick with some tits, Esther would take us. Trevor's parents were solid, and he seemed to have the most stable home out of all of us, but Trevor was anything but stable.

He had a Polaroid instant camera that he got a lot of use out of. He took photos of about 15 girls in middle school who posed for him in the nude. He had them spreading everything under the sun, and they seemed to enjoy it. At that time, I was wondering how in the hell could a guy in the ninth grade get these girls to pose nude for him. The best word to describe Trevor was "perverted". This kid would be in the hallway at school and pull his "Johnson" out on a whim. You forever heard him bragging daily about his nine and I guess it was true because all of the young ladies wanted to see it.

I was sneaking around just to see topless women in magazines and here it was, I was actually friends with the biggest porn star in the neighborhood and he was only 14 years old. Shit, Trevor even had pictures of my girlfriend in the nude. When I saw that, I was absolutely overwhelmed. My girlfriend was telling me that she was a virgin and we would finally make a go at it on prom night, but from my perspective, she was a far cry from being innocent. At that time though, I was still very naïve. I still had a crush on a dancer from the television show, "Solid Gold". I don't know if you remembered that show, but there was a sister on that show that was absolutely gorgeous, otherwise, I actually hated the show's content.

As the year went on, I decided to give Trevor a little bit of his own medicine. I figured that since he was busy screwing around with everyone else's girlfriend, he did not have the time to spend with his own, so I started doing it for him. Irene and I were good friends and we wanted to hit Trevor where it hurt. After talking on the phone several times, we started meeting each other alone and would just hang out together to make him jealous.

The day that Trevor found out about our little fling, he retaliated on the school bus. We were getting ready to go at it, but as always, Randy stepped in and shortly after, things were back to normal between Trevor and me. Think about it, I said, the girls that he had the naked pictures of were freshmen in high school. If girls were doing that in the '80s when times were slower, imagine what your daughter could be doing.

Later that year, I decided that I would go to the prom. The prom was not really for eighth graders, but we could go if we wanted to. One would think that this would be a great time for me, but I actually had to go to the prom with my cousin Jackie. Jackie and I were the same age, but she was a grade ahead of me. She did not have a date, so I was recruited to accompany her that year. Also, Jackie had just had a baby for a guy who was out of high school, and everyone knew that he was not going to be around for long.

She was one of my favorite cousins, so how could I say no. I was also looking at it in another way. My cousin had some very good-looking friends and I knew that most of them would be there. This would be my chance to be the innocent, understanding gentleman and, perhaps, get rid of my virgin status. Sadly, many black men were not identified by their peers for how smart they were, they were simply identified by how much pussy they got, and I was not getting any.

You could be the most ignorant, disrespectful bastard known to man, but if you were getting some pussy, you were the envy of all your peers. Another status was clothes. You did not have to know how to spell Stacy Adams or baggies, but if you were wearing them, you were all of a sudden exalted into the Beaufort County's pimp of fame. The prerequisite to having this honor was having a jerry curl, a Lawrence Welk shirt, a pair of baggies, a pair of patent leather shoes, a Cutlass Supreme with dark-tinted windows, and of course you had to be getting or pretending to get lots of pussy. As the prom night came and went, my cousin and I actually had a pretty good time as she introduced me to most of her friends. I even kissed one of them on the cheek, but of course, I did not get to peel any panties. I still have the pictures from that prom and it is very funny to look at. My suit was absolutely ugly and my cousin was skinny and much taller than I was. One glance at that photo and you're able to tell that she was doing the taking and I was the guest. My suit looked like one of mother's homemade specials. Bless her heart, she made many of clothes, but that polyester material was not paying me any dividends. Being at the prom was easy, but getting out of the neighborhood with that suit on was a challenge as the older guys would rip into you once given the opportunity.

Supervision was minimal at best as many of the guys who were driving already were taking girls in their cars and leaving. My cousin and I simply waited on a relative to pick us up and we headed off home.

I had witnessed many things during the year that opened my eyes wide. I knew deep down inside that I was not like most of my friends because I had a genuine appreciation for people and cared about the hurt I would cause others by doing them wrong. I still wanted to hang around the cool crowd, but I found just as much joy listening to the old men talking under a tree on a hot summer day. I learned patience from watching Uncle Bill work on his fishing nets day after day on the porch, from watching Grandma Baybe construct a quilt out of scraps that most people would have thrown away, from watching Great Grandmother Dadah use the entire evening to clean 100 mullet fish that she was going to share with the rest of the family, and by listening to Great Grandmother Janie talk about how things use to be as we ate gingersnap cookies and drank that chest busting Royal Crown cola that I had to dilute with water as we sat on the porch. They seemed to never be in a rush when doing things; they just knew that with persistence and patience, the final product would eventually show itself. Once I entered the ninth grade at Robert Smalls, I seemed to come into my own. With the help of Trevor, that summer had finally relieved me of my virgin status. Though everyone thought that I was well seasoned, I had still just conquered one female at the age of 15. When it came to kissing, I had my share of that, but I was never one for pushing the issue when it came to sex. I appreciated other things, like being in the band and playing basketball, especially since I was known as the best player at the school.

In the '60s, Robert Smalls was an all-black school that my parents had gone to, so it had a lot of history in Beaufort County. Mr. Drew was the band director at Robert Smalls, and again I would meet another black man that would influence my life in a positive way. We would have concerts, go to football games, and frequently be invited to parades all over the state. Our band had a reputation of being one of the best bands in the entire state.

Mr. Drew appealed to me because of his love for young people. We were young adults who were still trying to find out where we fit in within society, and Mr. Drew understood that. Most of us had hormones growing wild, and he knew just what to say or do to put it all in perspective. It seemed as if he could see into the future. He used to tell us which girls would be most successful, and as it turned out, he was right on the money. It is funny how older people can see these things. Also, most of the girls who had the great bodies are now over 200 pounds, and the ones who were as skinny as sticks and wore Coke bottle glasses turned out to be gorgeous. To my surprise, Mr. Drew was also a student of Mr. Douglas, my first band director.

Once I knew that, I knew that he had a sincere appreciation for young people of all color and had our best interest at heart. That year, I met a girl who was in the eighth grade, and I thought that she was the most beautiful girl that I had ever laid eyes on. She already had a reputation for being with men, but I didn't care. It was hard to tell how much of that stuff was actually true. How much sex could a girl in the eighth grade have actually experienced in her short life? Her name was Courtney and once I met her, I just knew that I had to have her. She had a very beautiful complexion and silky long hair. I introduced myself to her one day after I had just finished one of my band sessions. The previous summer had given me the confidence I needed to approach young women, and I knew that I wanted this one. Courtney already knew who I was, and to my surprise, she told me that she was trying to figure out a way to say something to me. We would become very close that school year, and I even went to her home a few times to visit. Her mother was a schoolteacher at the high school and I could tell that she did not want me around when she first got a glimpse of me. Courtney was small, cute, and looked innocent. I looked very rugged, I was already shaving, and I seemed very sure of myself. I was starting to branch out a little on the wild side. I joined the basketball team and all of a sudden, I was in the spotlight and known by many from the other schools. I was even known at the high school that I would attend the following year. People would come to watch me play and it made me feel good to see Courtney in the stands while I was doing my thing. To my surprise, I was voted the most popular male at the entire school. From grades one to nine, I had made significant progress in the confidence department. I had many friends that were not jealous at all of what I was doing. As a matter of fact, they could always count on me to do something wild if I thought we would not get caught and it did not endanger anyone's life. Oh yeah, I did some crazy shit that my mother would have killed me for if she knew that I had done them. Before basketball practice, we would be bored to death because we had to wait outside the gym until the girls' team had finished practicing. The girls' team was coached by a teacher named Ms. Dunns. She did not like any of us because she thought that we all were criminals. Some of the guys on the team actually were, but to put us all in the same pot was wrong. Ms. Dunns was a mother figure to all of the young girls and a bitch to the young guys.

She pretty much saw to it that none of us would come near those girls. We often wondered about her sexual preference because she was shaped mostly like a man. She had to have had the worst body I had ever seen on a woman in my 15 years of existence. To say that she was shaped like a Popsicle was an understatement. All of the teachers at the school were definitely not like that. You had Mrs. Chauncey who wore her pony tail to work with her pumps and she was absolutely breath taking. She was the study hall teacher and every young man signed up for study hall whether you needed it or not. Ms. Dunns was on the other side of the spectrum when it came to looking sexy.

The fellas and I would just get bored and try to find something to do to keep us busy until we could get inside the gym. My friend Andy, who we called Daddy Frog, was notorious for breaking into the cafeteria where we would take milk, food, and every other thing that we could find. There was also my friend Hamm. Hamm really did not give a shit what we did as long as it was interesting and he profited. One day, we decided to play around on one of the school buses that was left on the school yard. Hamm found some keys in the ashtray on the bus. Before I knew it, Hamm's crazy ass cranked up the school bus and off we went. We took it for a spin for about 15 minutes before we parked it. Ms. Dunns saw us just as the girls' basketball practice was about to come to an end. Of course she reported us the next day, but the break for us was the fact that we were at a distance and she could not correctly identify us as the perpetrators that took the bus. We were worried a little that one of the guys from the team would tell. Most of the guys on the team did not give a shit about anything, but one of the guys whose name was Ely did not believe in doing that type of thing. Ely was considerably older than all of us, as I think he was about 18 in the ninth grade, but he kept his mouth closed and said that he did not see anything. I knew that that was the last time I was going to pull some dumb shit like that. Everyone has a little gangster in them. Some folks dream of outrunning the cops or robbing a bank, but most of us don't have the balls to go through with it.

By the end of my freshman year at Robert Smalls, I was well educated in the do's and don'ts of life. I learned that women will come and go once they get bored and you lose a little of your celebrity status. Courtney and I had broken up, as it was someone else's turn to have her.

The last big school event of the year was the annual Memorial Day parade. Every high and middle school within a 30-mile radius was invited to participate in the parade.

This was like an annual meeting place for the local citizens. As a matter of fact, that was the only time that some folks actually saw each other. You never had to guess who had the best band. Out of ten bands and thousands of people, the one person you always looked for was Tootie.

Tootie was somewhat of a folk hero in the community. All of the bands would start at the Greyhound station and wait for Tootie to make his mark. If Tootie chose your band, it was going to be your day. That meant that you were going to strut a little harder and play a little harder. Tootie was always about five paces ahead of the majorettes, and by the time we made the turn by the bridge, you could hear the people start to scream his name. This went on until we came to the finish line. Tootie would do his dance, and the crowd would just lose their fucking minds. The rest of the world had Michael Jackson, but our hero was a handicapped 50-year-old named Tootie. At the end of the parade, everyone would rush to the end of the courtyard where your differences had to be settled. No one brought a gun, knife, or even raised their hands to touch anyone.

See, this was the time when the audience had to judge who truly had the best drummers in the county. The battle of the bands always had to end with the percussion section facing each other from rival schools. We were always ready, as we had a kid named Eddie leading the way. We called him "Cool Breeze" because he would beat the shit out of those drums, and it seemed as if he would not even break a sweat.

"Cool Breeze" would listen to the Eagles from the rival school tap their drums, and they would initially have the upper hand, but then he would raised his quad drums that seemed to weigh more than he did and beat the shit out of them until they would burst. We got great satisfaction out of that because we knew that we had just kicked their asses two times. The fact that we were not yet in a traditional high school made it just that more impressive.

As we said our good-byes for the summer, we knew that we were about to enter the big time of finally getting to high school. A few of us had already had a taste of going to Battery Creek during the year. Battery Creek had a Junior Varsity basketball team, and if you were good enough, you could play with them once the season was over at Robert Smalls Middle School. There were two of us who made the cut. It was very interesting because we got to spend about two months with the team and traveled throughout the state with the varsity girls' and boys' teams. With that experience fresh in my mind, I knew that Battery Creek High would be very challenging at first because all of the celebrity status that I had built up at Robert Smalls would not mean shit as a tenth grader at Battery Creek. I would just be another young buck who was trying to find his way at a new school.

CHAPTER 7
SUMMER JOBS

During the summer of 1982, I grew up by leaps and bounds. I was starting to hang out with some of the older guys in the neighborhood who had no problems getting into the mix. I found a job on the Marine Corps air station, which was about five miles away from my house. Though I had my driver's license and a willingness to be to work on time, it was kind of hard to find a steady ride to work. I solved that problem by borrowing my cousin Veronica's bike for the summer.

The job was part of a school program called Comprehensive Employment and Training Act (CETA). This program offered summer jobs to low income high school students. It paid shit and was more like slavery, but the previous year, I babysat my brother and my neighbor's son and decided that anything would be better than to go through that for another summer. CETA had many summer jobs for poor black souls like me who needed to supplement the family's income on $3.50 an hour. The first job that I got was to lay tar on top of buildings. That job lasted only about two weeks. After looking in the mirror and not being able to distinguish my hairline from my hair, I knew that it was time to quit. Black is beautiful, but being a roofer in June in South Carolina makes your skin look like it has been spray-painted with a can of black paint. After that, I called CETA and they were compassionate enough to give me another position.

This time, I was able to get on with a forest ranger. My boss was kind of strange but he had a genuine love for animals. It sounded easy enough, all I had to do was go in the woods and set out food for the animals. I did this for two weeks before I started to realize a daily itch all over my body. As it turned out, I had been bitten by red bugs all over my body, and they were trying to eat me alive. When you are in the woods, bugs don't discriminate. They will bite you on your legs, back, arms, and even your balls.

When I showed them to my boss, Forest Ranger Bob, he looked at them as if it was an initiation. His exact words were, "Look at those boogers, they look nice." Are you fricken kidding me? Hey, I was a teenager. What girl was going to come around me when I had bumps all over my body? I was ready to quit, but this time, my mother called CETA to try to get me a different position. CETA decided that they would give me another chance and I could try my hand at another job. This time, I would be working at the base NCO club as a dishwasher.

When I scoped out this job, I knew that I was finally going to get a job that I could deal with, and perhaps I could stay on the job longer than two weeks. It was very simple.

All I had to do was scrape off a few dishes after people ate their breakfast and lunch and run them through the dishwasher. After that, we had to prepare the club for the night action. I was too young to patronize the club, but I was allowed to set up the alcohol and clean it. My partner was a white kid named Eddie who was 20 years old.

He was the head dishwasher and was very proud of that position. I looked at him and said, "head dishwasher of what?" You don't have anyone to supervise. Once I looked at him, loser was the first thing that entered my mind. He was nice enough, but he made no bones about who was actually in charge. I didn't give a shit, I was just happy to be out of the sun. He asked me how much I was being paid and when I said $3.50 an hour, a smile came over Eddie's face because he was making $3.75 an hour. Wow, a whole fucking quarter more an hour. It was at that precise moment that I knew something better in life was in store for me. I was not going to screw up my opportunity to make a couple of dollars, but once I received a few paychecks to buy some things, I knew that I would leave Eddie with his dishwashing duties all to himself.

The first week went by with a breeze. After breakfast, Eddie and I would meet the beer truck to unload the beer and move it from the freezer to the bar. We had to finish dealing with the alcohol by a certain time of the day because both of us were underage and were not supposed to be handling alcohol. One day as we were moving some beer to one of the freezers, Eddie lost it and started going into spasms. I almost freaked out and was about to leave to get help, but then Eddie came to his senses and stopped me. I asked him what the fuck was going on, and he replied that sometimes he caught seizures. He also informed me that the boss told him that if he caught one more seizure, he was going to have to fire him for safety reasons. At this point, it occurred to me that Eddie really could not get any other job because his seizures were just too violent. It also occurred to me that Eddie was not going to mess with me because I could make up a seizure story at any time. From that time on, we were equal partners in every way, except for the fact that he made an extra quarter an hour. To my advantage, though, I did not have to scrape all of the dried egg yolks off of the plates while Eddie just watched anymore. I did not have to listen to him telling me to run the plates, knives, and forks through the dishwasher again when I knew he was just doing it because he was in charge. Most of all, I did not have to get up and get his fat ass a glass of soda when he was already near the soda machine. I knew in my heart that it was not right to hold a sickness over someone's head, but at that time, that is all I had to keep Eddie at bay.

One day after a few more weeks had passed by and I was contemplating quitting, Eddie and I were just sitting in the pool hall shooting the breeze when out of nowhere, one of his violent seizures started. He was knocking down everything in sight, and though I was pretty strong, Eddie weighed about 230 pounds and I could not control him.

Unfortunately for him, the boss was right there with a bird's eye view of the entire episode. Eddie was called in the office immediately and was fired. I had learned the ropes by then, so it was easy to let Eddie go.

The only problem I saw with the current situation was that I knew I was not going to be employed there myself for much longer. I had already put away a few checks and managed to buy myself a few threads with the money my mother let me keep. If nothing else, Eddie made me feel better about myself. After Eddie and I had said our good-byes, the boss called me into his office and made me his head dishwasher.

Wow! What a fucking joke that was. To add more insult to this meaningless job, I did not even have anyone to supervise. The crook did not even give me my extra quarter an hour because he said that was something he would have to take up with CETA. So in essence, since the government was paying me, he had free labor for the rest of the summer.

As I rode my cousin's bike home that day on Highway 21, I was calculating in my head as to what would be the right time to quit. I also was thinking about how my mother would get on my case if I were to just quit another job.

I mean, all of my jobs up to now had always ended with me quitting. I was a bag boy at a grocery store called Piggly Wiggly, but I quit because I wanted to play basketball instead. Furthermore, I was a lousy bag boy who was notorious for smashing a few loaves of bread and breaking eggs. I was a roofer, but I refused to look like the tar I was actually putting on the roof. I thought it should have been against the law for anyone to have a job as a roofer in South Carolina in June. If the weather was 95 degrees outside, you could of added an additional 20 degrees to the roof. You could of marked my arm with a sharpy and not be able to see it. I was a forest ranger assistant, but I itched so bad that the fellas in the neighborhood thought that I had the crabs. If nothing else, I had to keep this dishwashing job until the summer ended just to prove to myself that I could actually hold on to one. What else was I going to do for the summer. All of the unemployed guys in the neighborhood just sat under the unemployment tree smoking reefer, drinking Olde English 800s, and thinking about their next gig.

Most of them just got a hustle when they could and did not really want to get on anyone's payroll. Many of them had child support issues and knew that if they had gotten a job, they would have to pay more. If you did not have a job, child support could range anywhere from 30 to 50 dollars a month. Some of them could not even pay that. It never occurred to them that if they were not paying taxes, they would never get anything out of social security. The ones that it did occur to did not expect to live that long to benefit from it anyway. When they had gotten home from a stint in jail, they would brag about who they had seen and how that person was doing. They made it sound as if they were on vacation and met their long lost relative at a family reunion. Amazingly, though, most of them had old cars that they had hooked up. Initially, they would pay for the title, tags, and insurance, but would never make another payment after that. You knew that if you were going to get in the car with one of those cats, there was a probability that you could end up in jail because they were never going to just settle with being pulled over by a cop. When the lights came on to pull those dudes over, the chase was on. If they could make it to the neighborhood, more than likely, they were going to escape. Those guys knew the back roads and many of the cops did not dare come in the hood to chase those guys in the bottoms. Once they were released, the brothers never hesitated to let you know how fucked up the white man was. It was the white man who made you impregnate that woman so you would have to pay child support. It was the white man who made you buy that car and not put insurance on it. It was the white man who made you drop out of school in the tenth grade because you felt like you could not handle it anymore. It was the white man who made you lose all of your money gambling before you brought one red cent home to your family.

White people have done some bad shit in this world, but if you think for once that a person has your best interest at heart just because they are the same color as you are, you are bullshitting yourself. There are only two kinds of people in this world, good ones and bad ones.

I told my mother about the firing of Eddie at dinner, and she stressed to me the importance of finishing the job for the summer so I could have something to fall back on during the school year. The next day, I started my own routine as I found out that I could actually get the job done faster by myself and Eddie's lazy ass was just slowing me down. I was about 160 pounds and full of energy. On the other hand, Eddie's fat ass needed to rest about every ten minutes when we were working. He would sweat so much after about 30 minutes that it looked like he had gone swimming fully clothed. I was meeting lots of people and learned how to shoot pool during my break time. I figured that that was the least the boss could do because with CETA paying for me to be there, he did not have to come out of pocket for anything. He also made sure that I had plenty of food and refreshments at my leisure. Why not keep me happy? I was just another fatherless black kid looking for a job, and surely I was lucky to be in the position that I was in. When the last day arrived, the boss called me into the office to have a talk with me. He wished me well for the upcoming school year and said that if I needed a job for the next summer, I could come back and work for him. I knew that when I walked out of that door that day, my dishwashing days would come to a halt. When I asked him who he was getting to replace me since he did not have a dishwasher anymore, he mentioned Eddie. He knew that I could manage by myself, so the seizures were just an excuse to lay Eddie off until I started school. As I was walking through the door for the last time, there he was all grins and smiles. Eddie looked at me and said, "I knew he would ask me to come back." He was even dumber than I thought because he did not understand that the only reason he was back was because I was leaving and no one else wanted that shitty job.

Finally, I finished a summer job and felt like I had accomplished something. For the rest of the summer, I pretty much did what every typical high school boy does. I played sports, drank beer, and chased behind girls. To do anything else would require me to be a hermit. If I was riding in the car with Trevor, I knew that we would be trying to get into some X-rated movie that we would not ordinarily be allowed to get into. My other partner Randy, who was the son of a preacher, was a little more reserved and laid back. Most people knew him as a gentleman. If I had to give a description of those two, most thought that Randy could have been somewhat of a Denzel Washington, while Trevor had the distinct look of Sammy Davis Jr. I also hung out with my cousin AJ who was five years older than I. AJ was like the big brother I never had. AJ was the one who taught me how to whistle, shoot a gun, smoke a joint, and play basketball. When we were small, he would steal a gun and we would shoot windows out of abandoned houses. No one ever knew that we had that gun. As we grew older, AJ changed his style and was one of the coolest cats on the block. His jerry curl was done to perfection. He always wore a fresh pair of baggies with new patent leather shoes.

For a while, I thought that he had problems with his legs because he had a cane to match every outfit. When we rode around, it did not take long before AJ fired up a joint.

AJ was a very smart individual, but he chose to use his smarts in the wrong way. AJ could have easily made it in the business world or even be a teacher, but he chose to teach me how to blow "shotguns" with a joint. As it goes, he was the best basketball player that I had ever laid eyes on, and there were no two people on our side of town who could take us on the court. If you thought that you were having a good day on the basketball court, you knew that it was coming to an end as soon as AJ and I showed up.

AJ's last words to me before I went to Battery Creek High were not to quit like he did because he knew that I had potential. He managed to make it all the way to grade twelve before he decided to call it quits. Though AJ had some faults like all of us, he was always there to talk to when I needed an older male to confide in.

CHAPTER 8
LEARNING THE ROPES

The time was finally here. I was to arrive at Battery Creek High School. It was really nothing to fear as I would be riding the bus with many people I knew from the neighborhood. From grades one through nine, there was always an adult who was driving the school bus and demanded respect. The tenth grade brought on new challenges in that department. Somehow, some smart ass figured that bus drivers who were the same age as the students could control them and make them sit down and be quiet when they were told. There was a little of everything happening on the bus. Some kids were making out, some were throwing things out of the window, and some were just intimidating others by "checking" them. You could figure out who the weak people were the very first day. "Checking" someone is when you talk about their unemployed father, fat mother, whoring sister, gay brother, dope addict uncle, or the ugly cheap clothes that they are wearing. It is silly, but most of us enjoyed the laughs we got from it. In a nut shell, most of us who were on that bus were poor black kids who were fatherless and trying to find our own niche in life. It made some feel good to belittle others because their lives were just shit. Once someone starts to check you and you don't respond, you are going to be ridiculed for the entire school year. My cousin Carl who was all of 5 feet 2 inches tall, was the master "checker" on the bus and had the loudest mouth. Since I grew up with him and knew him very well, I received a pass but he tortured the hell out of the kids who lived in the other neighborhoods. If someone started to check you, you had to be prepared to retaliate or be subjected to their wrath for the entire school year. It was better to engage in a "check" and lose, than not to retaliate at all. No one and no subjects were off- limits. The first week of school proved how fucked up our priorities were as everyone sported their new rags and shoes that they worked all summer for. Instead of going to school to get a good education, most of the kids went to school just to see what the other kids were wearing. I was way ahead of the game in that respect, because I really never gave that much thought to clothes. If I had a clean pair of sneakers, a pair of jeans, and a nice shirt, I was good to go. If you started school with the same clothes that you had the previous year, that was grounds for checking. If you came to school with old shoes, you were also going to be checked. If your pants were not a solid color, that would require a checking immediately.

Someone would yell that you were wearing white man's pants, and it would be on. I remember when my mother, who made clothes, made me a pair of pants with no back pockets. Needless to say, I never wore those pants again after wearing them one day to school. You never knew what the checking was going to be about from day to day, but it was believed that men were not supposed to be wearing pants with no back pockets.

Someone forgot to tell my mother that. One day as we were going to school, one of the guys decided that he was going to check the bus driver. The bus driver, who was a senior, was not going to have any of it and decided to retaliate by checking from the driver's seat.

After the bus driver got the best of the guy who initiated the checking, the guy decided that he was going to kick the bus driver's ass right on the spot as he drove the bus. Instead of waiting until we got to the school where he could report it to the principal, the bus driver decided to turn the bus around and go to his cousin's house. His cousin, who had already dropped out of school a few years earlier, came on the bus and started to threaten the guy who initiated the check. Everyone was silent until the bus driver's cousin left the bus. As the bus driver drove away, he had to deal with the entire bus for being a punk and going back to his cousin's house for help. I was always a person who saw reasoning behind everything, and though the driver did not have any balls, I refused to harass him and urged some of the other guys to leave him alone. Besides, I was on the damn bus and I did not want this guy to lose it. As it turned out, turning that bus around and going to his cousin's house was wise because the principal could not guarantee his protection, but his cousin could and would.

Usually everyone got to school and hung around the cafeteria area whether they were eating or not. That is where the ladies hung out and you could see who was wearing the latest fashions. We thought that we had a little status, but each and everyone of us had meal passes. They gave us this small square meal pass for the month and one of the cooks would punch a small circled hole in it as we went through the line. I still don't understand the procedures for punching the holes in the meal card because there was absolutely no uniformity to it.

Some of the holes went straight down the middle, while some went up and down diagonally. Still others went in a circular motion on the meal card. We knew that they did not have a clue to what they were doing, so we tested the system. We would go through the breakfast and lunch lines several times to see if we would be rejected and it never happened.

Either the cooks did not know any better or they thought that maybe we were not getting enough food at home and it was just going to be thrown away anyway. One day as I was just standing at the usual "checking" spot near the cafeteria, a girl named Sally came over and said that she wanted to talk to me for a minute. I never paid Sally much attention through the years because I always thought that she was not the sharpest knife in the drawer. After the ninth grade summer, Sally had filled out.

She went from this dingy-looking girl with braces to this very attractive and tall young lady. When she said that she wanted to talk to me about something, I thought that she had her eyes on me and wanted to get to know me better.

Sally asked me to follow her outside because she wanted to introduce me to someone. When we got to our destination on the other side of the building, I was startled as she introduced me to her older stepsister, who was gorgeous. Sally's exact words were, "Chris, I want to introduce you to Terri." What puzzled me more was the fact that I knew all of the girls that came from Robert Smalls Middle School and didn't recognize this one. When I looked at her again, she was already developed in all areas, so I knew she could not be a sophomore. Once we looked at each other, I was speechless. I needed to know where she was from and what she wanted with me. When I looked around, Sally was gone and it was just the two of us standing there. I had never been in awe of a girl before, but this time I was completely overwhelmed. After I introduced myself, Terri politely told me that she had seen me around the school grounds and just wanted to know me. Still pretty much speechless, I thanked her and found a way to escape that situation until I could compose myself. The next day, I managed to get her phone number and started to call her. It was easier on the phone because I did not have to look into her eyes. I did not have to act confident while all the time breaking out in a sweat. We discussed several things, and before you knew it, she was my girlfriend in school.

At the time, I was the brunt of many jokes because it was unheard of for a senior to be interested in a sophomore. Terri was a senior and I was the little sophomore who she was just going to play with until the school year ended.

Many of the girls who were in high school just got bored with the guys in their class and saw the freshmen as new meat coming to the school. I really didn't care because if I could be with a senior, my popularity and status would be on the rise. I knew Terri would not take me too seriously, and Trevor and the rest of the fellas told me that there was absolutely no way I was ever going to get in those panties. The way I looked at it, I did not have to get anything from her because to be in her presence was all I needed. My plan was to use the chicken heads if I needed sex and have Terri as my true lady. I figured I could get away with that, until one day Terri told me that she loved me and gave me a kiss outside of the lunchroom. My entire game plan changed at that instant because now she was also telling me that I could come over to her house to visit. I was not too keen about going to any female's house because once their parents found out who my father was, I was pretty much out the door. Though years had passed by, my father was still a shit-talking, dope-smoking, woman-beating, liquor-drinking asshole who did not mind tearing up shit, and you know what they say, "The apple don't fall too far from the tree." I just knew that once her father got wind that I was Shane's son, he was going to get a restraining order on me to stay away from his daughter. Who could blame him? I had never met a single man who had anything good to say about my father. Even his own father thought that he was pretty much worthless.

Once Terri introduced me to her father, I had trouble looking him in his eyes. A rule of thumb to follow is to always look a man in his eyes. If you cannot look him directly in his eyes, look at his eyebrows and most of the time, they will never know the difference. When Terri's father asked me who my parents were, I had to tell him the truth. I was safe on my mother's half of the family, but once he identified me as Shane's son, I thought he was going to kick me out on the spot. My father was constantly raising hell while going in and out of jail. He would also brag about how many women's asses he had kicked during the week. The rumor about my grandfather was that he had just recently killed someone also, so nothing was going to help me on my father's side. It did not help that he was also jailed recently for driving drunk on the wrong side of the road while having an expired driver's license.

Terri lived alone with her father, and the last thing he wanted was for me to go upside his daughter's head. I had no intentions of doing that, but how would he know that? I was Shane's son. How could he know that I was a perfect gentleman and did not have that kind of aggression in me? To his credit, he did not kick me out or talk bad about my father, but he did warn his daughter about who my father was. For the first time in my entire life, I felt that I belonged to one woman and that was the only woman that I wanted to be with. I did not screw around with other girls and did not even talk to them on the telephone. Yeah, I was with the woman that I wanted to be with. You can tell when a guy's nose is wide open. He starts to do dumb shit that otherwise he would never do. My twin cousin Angie lived approximately two miles away from Terri's house, so I started to make up excuses to spend a few nights with her, knowing my mother would not mind. While there, I would run to Terri's house and stay there until her father was about to come home. We would be in her room buck naked with sex in the air, and all of a sudden, her father would be backing his long van into the driveway. She would always jump up and start throwing my clothes at me to get them on.

I would be laughing the entire time. It was something about the danger of being caught that gave me a sick thrill. I knew that if he had caught me in bed with his daughter, I would not live to tell about it the next day. I always somehow managed to get my clothes on just in the nick of time. I figured her father knew what was going on, but he figured that he would leave well enough alone as long as he never saw anything. I also knew that nothing would change his mind about me. Her father did not care for me and I could see it in his eyes. It did not help that one of his friends who he had recently bought some land from was telling him that I was no good and that his daughter was making a major mistake by getting involved with the likes of me. They all thought that Terri deserved to be with a doctor, lawyer, or someone who was a lot better than I was. Maybe he saw a lot of himself in me and really did not like himself. For whatever reasons, Terri could not get enough of me and refused to let me go. I guess the saying that nice girls love boys who are a little on the rough side is true.

Once the weekend came, things were a little different. Saturday was a time for baseball, cookouts, and family gatherings. My family would always find a reason to throw a party. By Saturday morning, you had to decide whose party you were going to attend. The reasons were plenty for having a party. Some would have a party just to raise the money for rent. There might be a party to get someone out of jail. You might just have a party to get someone's repossessed car back, or simply throw a party because you did not have shit else to do. The menu always read the same. You would have some red rice, hog maw soup, fried fish, fried chicken, fried pork chops, potato salad, and probably a damn deer that someone had donated to the party.

If you wanted your fried meat between some bread, that required an additional 50 cents. There was always a wide assortment of beverages to choose from at these parties. There was malt liquor, wild Irish rose, Seagram's gin, Smirnoff whiskey, and of course, your moonshine, which was also called scrap iron. If something is called "scrap iron," you know that it is lethal. Everyone had their own different variety of scrap iron. You had straight scrap, plum scrap, raisin scrap, cranberry scrap, and lemon scrap. You knew you had a good bottle of scrap iron if you shook the bottle and the bubbles stayed to the top of the jar for a couple of seconds. If you drank it too fast, you would have a problem waking up the next day. Scrap iron was definitely sipping whiskey and nothing an amateur should play with.

Saturday nights were just an extension of Fridays for the diehard weekend partygoers. They did not care what they had to do—they were going to be at the party. Some women who could not find babysitters would simply bring their children with them to the party. Those parties with alcohol and drugs were actually no place for a child to be. My cousins and I were always at the parties with our parents when I was very small growing up. No one wanted to miss anything in those days and stay home, so they just brought the damn kids with them. There were also various parties throughout the county that you had to choose from. The decision depended on your favorite Disc Jockey. You had "Bread Man Dee, Mr. Magic, Kid Boogie, Pee Wee & Bamm Bamm, Kenny "hip shaking" Murphy yelling, "Tooooonight", or Bobby Nichols". You could be at "Smalls Paradise, The Hut, Studio Seven, or just simply at the neighborhood club, "Lolimay"s. You did not need a radio station or fancy adds put in the paper to get the information across. All you needed was a few big damn cardboards, some nails, and a tree near the highway. That was advertisement at its finest in the hood.

Sunday was a day of worship for most of the family as we headed out to Second Grays Hill Baptist church. The church was very small, but it was family-oriented and had a sense of home. My great grandmother Dadah was always the family leader at church. Since that was the church Dadah was affiliated with, no one dared belong to another church. No one missed church Sunday. Dadah's seat was always in the front row on the left side of the pew. Sitting next to Dadah or behind her were three generations of family. All of the women had to have their heads covered. Everyone also had to have on their Sunday's best.

During the week, most black people did not have a job where they could put on a suit or don a beautiful dress. Sunday was the only time to show off that fancy dress that you had in the closet. Most of the time, the kids were bored as the Reverend Jacobs would preach his sermon. He was very charismatic and charming. People loved his preaching so much with that deep raspy voice of his, they would come from miles around just to hear him talk and sing. For me, church always seemed to interfere with football. In the south, black folks love to stay in church the entire day. I would be in church looking at my watch and wondering what was going on with the football games. To extend the time, food would be served after the church service. If you did not have a good meal for the entire week, you could guarantee yourself that there was going to be some good food at church. All of the ladies were required to bring a dish, and everything was eaten because the ladies only brought their best. The food consisted of collard greens with neck bones or ham hocks, cabbage with pig tails, yams, macaroni with that free government cheese, potato salad, macaroni salad, red rice with smoked sausage, white rice, fried chicken, fried fish, sweet potato pie, pumpkin pie, cake, and refreshments. There were no limits to how much you could eat. If you ate until you burst, the adults were happy. By the time I got home on a Sunday evening, I was just interested in watching the rest of the football games and getting myself prepared for another week at Battery Creek.

CHAPTER 9
COMPETITION

As the months passed by on yet another year of school, I was faring pretty darn well. I made the varsity basketball team, though I rode the pine for most of the year. I had the most beautiful girl at the school, and my grades were pretty good. It seemed as if the year just flew by, but that is what happens when you are having fun. Before I knew it, it was time for me to take Terri to her senior prom. Though the prom was open to everyone at the school, I knew that I would be in the minority by being the only sophomore there, but she told me that it would be alright. I bought a new suit and was ready to go. I was proud of the fact that I could go to Martin men's shop and purchase a new suit. Up until then, I only had Sweetwater suits that my mother had made for me. When we arrived at the prom, my eyes were wide open as I had made it to the big show. Think about it—I was at the prom with a girl that many guys wanted and I was only a sophomore. We savored the moment by holding each other all night. The feeling was great, after all of the obstacles I thought I would have to encounter, Terri still wanted to be by my side. After we said our good-byes, we decided to go and grab a bite to eat. Things were going smooth, but I did not plan my finances correctly. As we finished our food, I noticed that I did not have any more cash. Normally this would not be a problem, but my gas tank was almost empty. After thinking that I had planned everything perfectly, how could I be so stupid as to not have enough money to purchase gas.

There was no time to be macho, so I decided to ask Terri for a loan to put some gas in the tank. I knew she had some cash because her father would never send her on a date without money to get home. Plus she was one of those types of girls that Daddy gave 50-dollar allowances to for waking up in the morning. As I stated earlier, most of the black kids at Battery Creek High school got free lunch, but Terri was in a different financial bracket and paid for her lunch. It was as if the people who paid was saying, "pardon me freeloaders, but I have to pay for my lunch because my father makes fifty thousand dollars a year and you have this coupon because you all are broke asses". I asked her for the loan to put gas in the tank, but she refused to give it to me. Gas was only about 88 cents a gallon, but she was not about to give a man money on prom night. Once the dust settled, she managed to give me a quarter. With nothing else to do, I scraped up two cents from under the seat and put 27 cents worth of gas in my mother's green 1975 Chevy Nova. The store clerk had the laugh of his life and so did Terri. I did not find it that amusing, but she still was not about to give me a dollar of her money. As I was driving back to my house, I was thinking that it was going to be over soon anyway because she was going to college and I was only a sophomore. Surely she would not continue a relationship with a guy in high school. I made sure that I only drove the car 40 miles an hour to conserve the 27 cents worth of gas I had just put in the car. You could always tell when that lime green Nova was in the area because you could smell it. Putting gas in the tank also required adding a quart of oil. I fixed that problem by going around the neighborhood to pick up old oil that people would take out of their cars. They did not have to worry about environmental waste, I was the oil pickup man for the neighborhood. If the oil was sitting in the rain, "no problem". If the oil had a little dirt on it, "no problem", If a dog just happened to piss in it, "no problem", call me because that oil was going to go in that lime green Nova. Once home, Terri and I talked for a while and she thanked me for the night. She mentioned to me that her senior trip was coming up and she needed money to go on the trip. Besides that, she wanted to know if I could come up with some spending money for her and explained to me that she really did not have any cash for gas. Hell, I didn't believe her, but like a sucker, I agreed even though I had absolutely no idea where I was going to get money from to give to her.

Anyway, I figured why was I going to give her money when I was broke as a joke and her father was rolling in dough? Wasn't I the guy who had to get the free lunch? It did not make any sense, but like a fool, I agreed to it. On the day of the senior trip, she calmly walked up to me and asked me for the money. I looked at her and told her that I had fallen on hard times and could not come up with the money. For sure, that was going to be it. After all, many other guys who had already graduated and some who were at school had much more to offer than I did. Why did she need a guy who did not have his own car, a job, and was only a sophomore? As she walked away, I knew it was over even though we did not officially break it off. The phone calls and visits came to a halt. I knew that this was the best thing and I had already gone as far as I could possibly go with Terri. If nothing else, she had given me the confidence that I could be with any woman that I wanted to be with.

After Terri, my school years seemed to go by like a blur. There were no exciting summer vacations with the parents or family picnics at the beach. The same routine would continue for the next two years. I would talk to a girl for a few months and then would get tired of her. My senior year was busy as I was the star basketball player at the school, a jazz musician, and even made the magazine of "Who's Who" in America. The future looked bright as I felt I could do anything that I wanted to do. Most of us were milling around with the colleges we were going to attend after high school. I was thinking very hard about college, but I knew in my heart that I was tired of school and needed a break. I had started seeing Kelly, who was a sophomore at the rival school Beaufort High. She was a pretty, dark-complected girl with big beautiful eyes. I never thought it would last, but what else did I have to do? The other girl who I was seeing at my school was not pretty when talking about pure beauty, but she had the nicest figure that could be given to a woman. When Joan walked, the guys just looked at her round figure, amazed that God could actually grace a 17-year-old with a body like that. She knew it as it seemed as if she was shaking her ass so hard, she was hitting lockers on both sides of the hall. Before the fellas confirmed their physical fitness class periods, they all had to find out which class Joan was in. I had no time to get into a serious relationship with anyone because I was still contemplating what I was going to do with my future. Most of the guys just wanted to take one day at a time and really had no immediate plans to leave home. If I was not sure about anything else in my life, I was sure that I did not want to live at home for another year. I loved my mother dearly, but her constant bickering had worn my nerves thin, and I was going to do whatever I had to do to escape that small town of Seabrook in Beaufort County. I was able to work a little on some side jobs and get money here and there from both my mother and my grandparents. I knew that college was not going to be a picnic as I would need the help and support from my family. My mother was urging me to get a job at a motel on Hilton Head, and I think that I was about to wear out my welcome with my grandfather when it came to borrowing money. I had to make a decision, so one day when the armed forces recruiters came to the high school, I decided to talk to them. Kelly's stepfather was a recruiter and he was talking to me about the benefits of the Army. When the black males in the neighborhood joined the military, all of them went into the Army. The Army seemed very typical for African-Americans, so I dismissed it immediately. I was already in Beaufort County where Parris Island, home of the United States Marines was, so I also knew that there was no way in hell I was going to join the Marine Corps. It seemed like the Air Force and the Navy had the best education and opportunity for what I was interested in. I would let fate decide which branch of service I was to go in. On the day of the Armed Forces examination, I waited on the outside of the office and decided that I would take the test of the first branch that showed up. The Navy came to work that morning before the Air Force did, and my decision was made. I took the Navy examination and felt confident that I had passed it with flying colors. It was amazing to me that a person could actually fail the test. After a few weeks, the Navy recruiter called me to tell me about the news and we discussed the delayed entry program. Once I told my mother about my decision, she was visibly upset and wondered why I had picked a racist organization with known gay people. I figured that many leaders of our country, including John F. Kennedy, had served in the Navy and no one ever told me that they were gay. I had remembered when John F. Kennedy said, "When asked what I have contributed in my lifetime, I can proudly say that I served in the United States Navy." I also told some of the guys in the neighborhood of my decision to join the United States Navy, but they looked at me as they smoked their joints and said, "Man, ain't no damn black man go join no fuckin' Navy. Have you lost your damn mind?" Another went on a little further by adding that they would send my black ass home within a month because they don't want any black southern boys in the United States Navy, especially one with a Gullah background and an island accent. After that, I did not want to discuss my decisions with anyone because I felt like I did not have the support at the time. I signed on for the delayed entry program to report to basic training in San Diego on 20 September 1985.

As the school year came to an end, Kelly and I were having some fun. She was an only child and spoiled rotten. I knew there was no future in that relationship; besides, boot camp would arrive in a couple of months and I would be long gone anyway. I was the only one that knew my mind was already made up to go in the Navy. The more I thought about my other options, the more I knew that the Navy was the best option for me. Even Kelly's stepfather, who was an Army recruiter, was telling me that when 300 Navy men go out to sea, 150 couples come back to port. I did not know about all of that, but I did know that I did not just want to be another black face joining the Army like the rest of my friends. My college support was minimal though I had won a music scholarship to Elizabeth City State College in North Carolina. My mother was constantly talking to me about getting a job nearby on Hilton Head island. Beaufort County was hopelessly bad when it came to working, as unemployment was very high, so everyone and their momma took the 45-minute to an hour commute to Hilton Head. About 30 years earlier, most of the land on Hilton Head belonged to blacks whose fathers were sharecroppers and fisherman. Some white genius decided that the land was a waste and it was a great place to build some golf courses. There was one problem with his idea. The Island of Hilton Head was the only place that most of the black people who lived there knew, and they were not willing or able to relocate. In essence, the money to buy the land from the black people who were on it meant nothing as they were not offered enough and did not have a plan to go elsewhere. Well, if there is a clause to fuck over black people and Indians, surely the government will think of it, and they came up with a good one. Why not just raise the land tax on their black asses so they cannot pay it and force them to leave? This was a great idea as one black family after another started to lose their property because of high land taxes. Once a few black people started seeing what was happening, it was not hard to convince them to sell their property for under market value or risk losing their property and get nothing for it. Before you knew it, there were golf courses and new developments everywhere. Segregation did not play a part in this as blacks still had access to the land, only now instead of living on it, they mowed the grass, cleaned the hotels, and washed the windows. It's funny because the black folks in the area didn't even see it coming.

Every day, hundreds of black folks around the county would

catch buses or carpool to Hilton Head just to go to a minimum wage job. I don't fault anyone for wanting to work, because I respect all people in all positions, regardless of status and education. I have always been taught that it's not the work that you do, but it is the pride that you take in completing the work. However, the way I saw it, they were no better off than the people who just stayed home all day. By the time they paid for their lunch and gas for the week on a two-hour-a-day commute and on a minimum wage salary, it really was not worth it. I knew that I was not going to spend the rest of my life subjecting myself to that bullshit, so every time my mother would suggest that I find a job on Hilton Head, I just ignored it and thought about something else.

I graduated high school in June. It was a relief to get out of high school as much as I screwed around in class. The work was never hard once I put my mind to it, but I hated school. I had been in the damn thing for 13 years and did not want one more second of it. When my mother asked me what I planned to do for the summer, I told her that I was just going to chill until I went to boot camp. That was a very unpopular answer as she was trying to encourage me to find a job. That summer of 1985 was the last job that I was going to have in Beaufort County. I certainly was not going to call CETA's cheap ass, and I did not want some run of the mill job, so I decided to go to the unemployment agency myself. Besides, it was June and I knew that the job was only going to be about three months long.

I lucked out and was given a job as a painter for a realty company. I had a partner named Marvin who was a professional painter, and all I had to do was help him paint the insides and outsides of houses. Marvin was a Picasso with the paintbrush and sometimes we would complete an entire house in one day. This kept my mother happy and off of my back, so I just gave her half of my earnings. I knew that I had to stop painting by August because I needed time to myself to prepare mentally for boot camp. My mother still did not think that I was going through with joining the Navy. Why would she believe me? The farthest I had been away from home was Myrtle Beach, which was only about three hours away. How in the world did I think I was going to make it away from home without the support of my family? The question I was asking myself was how in the hell could I stay in Beaufort County for the rest of my life and not at least give myself a chance to see another part of the world? If I screwed up, so what—my hometown, which time had forgotten, would still be there when I returned. I mean really, my district didn't even have cable television and this was 1985. A family vacation consisted of going 25 miles to the nearest beach and eating some sandwiches before we had to come back home. I saw one of my grand aunts give her son a bottle of hot sauce for Christmas one year. The jerry curl was still on the rise. You were considered dressed up when you had on a shorts set with matching socks and hard shoes. Oh yeah, I knew that the only thing that would keep me there was death itself.

My mother constantly asked me how I liked the job and informed me that a major hotel on Hilton Head was calling me to work there. The more I ignored her, the more she was letting me know that this was a great opportunity and I should take it. I also had scholarship offers because of my music, but for some reason, she never would never talk about that. I could never forgive my father for beating the hell out of her, but I could finally understand how he could leave her. I loved my mother to death, but she made you want to just grab the nearest bottle of booze and drink until you just passed out. In her defense, I don't think she realized just how annoying she really was. Also, I am sure it wasn't just her. When you are a teenager, you really don't want to hear anyone's shit. Hormones are growing wild and you think that you have all of the answers to everything, so I am sure I was getting on her nerves just as much as she was getting on mine.

One day, Marvin had to go on emergency vacation for two weeks, so the boss told me that I could have the truck and I would be doing the job by myself. Disaster struck during the first week. My painting was no problem, but I was nowhere close to being as fast as Marvin because it was taking me all week to finish one house. The boss put the pressure on me to finish the houses quickly because he had clients that needed to move in. After that, I did not chip away any old paint or do any prep work. I just laid the damn thing on top of the old paint and tried to get away with it. The boss was so upset with me, he asked me if I knew anyone who could paint. I said yeah, me, but since you wanted your work so fast, this is what you get. He gave me until the end of the week and I was fine with that. It was the middle of August and I had only a little over a month left before it was time to head to boot camp.

Again, my mother was not too happy that I was not working, but at that point, I did not care. I had some major work to do. I had to make sure my system was clean of weed prior to entering the MEPS center. I had been smoking weed off and on since the tenth grade and never really quite kicked the habit. I knew that there was no addiction, but as long as I was around AJ and some of those other guys, I was not going to stop. I could not risk the chance of going to the MEPS center and being popped positive for marijuana. I went cold turkey from the weed, stopped drinking, and started running every day. I wanted to be in the best shape physically and mentally when I got to boot camp. One thing that I was not going to give up was women. As the saying goes, you can't live with them and you surely can't live without them.

Terri was in college by now and she would keep in touch with me on occasions. I still had her phone number because she would pop in sometimes as she went to her father's house. She made no bones about getting over me. She even showed up to my mother's house one day with passion marks all over her neck. I never really cared what she was doing, but to come to my house like that was a sign of disrespect and I really wanted to kick her ass at that point.

When the time came to leave, I was told by my recruiter not to take a lot of clothes because I would not need them. I phoned Terri at her college in Columbia, SC to tell her the day that I would be coming down there to be processed in the military. I met the recruiter with some other guys early that morning, and we were off to Columbia, which was going to take about two and a half hours.

Once there and after filling out tons of paperwork, the question of drugs came up. Of course, I said that I had never tried the stuff and just hoped that my six weeks of cleansing had paid off. This was it, I was only going to be there for two days before it was time to head to San Diego and get my chance to see something else. The processing center would give us a place to stay until it was time to leave, but amazingly, Terri footed the bill for a hotel, food, and gave me spending cash. I did not call home and no one tried to figure out exactly where I was. Those two days made me realize that if I was going to be with any woman, it was going to be Terri. Through it all, faith had it that she would be the very last female that I saw prior to going through the biggest challenge of my life—the United States Navy.

CHAPTER 10
BOOT CAMP

I arrived in San Diego on a cool and crisp fall day. Yeah, I had joined the Navy and I had to clear my mind of everything negative I was being told about it. I had to dismiss all of the myths that it was the most racist of the four services, and for every 300 sailors that went out to sea, 150 couples would come to port. Or, a sailor has a woman in every port. Initially, I learned that every word spoken by most people in the Navy was accompanied by profanity, hence the term "cursing like a sailor."

Intimidation was really not a factor because I felt that my childhood had prepared me for any hardship I was about to encounter in the Navy. I had a leg up on things, but I also was at a disadvantage of sorts. I was in great physical condition, so the exercise portion of boot camp was going to be easy. Of all the activities that I was involved in during my youth, swimming was not one of them.

Wow, why in the hell would someone join the Navy if they did not know how to swim? I felt like a real jackass, especially when I saw the 12-foot pool we were going to have to swim in to complete basic training. We were given one week to learn how to swim the length of the pool. If you failed the swim portion, it also meant that you failed basic training and you were going to go home. I saw this actually happening to people who could flutter kick, but they could not float on their backs and that is what the Navy wanted to see. The reasoning behind this is because if you fell in the ocean, you would not last very long trying to swim, but if you knew how to float on your back, you could float for hours if help did not arrive immediately. Knowing the men in my family, I knew that they would make up other reasons as to why I was sent home. It would be everything from pissing the bed, to being sent home for drugs. I knew that they were going to make a joke out of it, and that was something I was not prepared to deal with. I prayed about it, and after the third day, I was swimming and floating on my back from one end to the other. I was no Jacques Cousteau, but I swam well enough to get out of boot camp. I was never one who celebrated good fortune for too long because there was always something that would bring me back down to earth.

As I sat there in my barracks on one cool October day in 1985, I commenced to open my mail that I received from my family. Mail was a big deal because you were only allowed one phone call home per week. At that time, you had to decide whether that call was going to go to your mother or girlfriend and Mom always won when it came to my phone calls. As I sorted through my mail, I noticed that I had received one from Kelly. When I saw the address, I was surprised because I thought that the fling we had was over once I got on the plane headed for California. Kelly was very cool and we just used to hang out around the neighborhood and have a real good time.

Though we went to rival high schools, we often spent time together. I was not prepared for the news that I was about to receive from her. There must have been hundreds of words on the letter, but the only words that I saw said, "I am pregnant." I looked at it over and over to make sure that I was not imagining things. After it had sunk in, I started to feel light-headed, and for the first time in my life, I thought that I was going to faint. My knees buckled as I went to the window for air. I could not believe it. How could I be so irresponsible? I immediately told my company commander that I had a family emergency and needed to call home. I did not call Kelly. I called my mother to ask her if she had heard the news. If this was true, surely my people had heard about it already. My mother acknowledged that she had, and asked me if I was prepared to raise a child in this world. I was not even prepared to take care of myself, let alone a child. When I got back to my barracks, I was upset with myself that I had just become another statistical young black man who was fathering a child and not prepared to take care of it. All along, I was writing and calling Terri because I knew that she was the one for me. Terri was pretty much no nonsense and knew what direction she wanted to go in life. At the time, Kelly was attending her junior year in high school and still was not taking anything seriously. My mother assured me that I was not the only person in this world who had done such an irresponsible thing and I would not be the last. I guess she could relate because she was only 15 years older than I was, but I did not want the same experience for myself. I knew how she struggled and the trials and tribulations she had to go through, and I did not want to face the same challenges. I thought that I could tell Terri about this and hope to keep our relationship intact, but I knew that she would not want to hear about that situation and it would prove that her father was right about me all along. I had to tell her, and when I did, just like that it was over. I thought that my life was over even before I had a chance to get it started. If this was a baseball game, it would have been a route. My life was shit and I knew it.

I started to tell myself that Kelly was not such a bad person and maybe, just maybe, I could learn to love her also. Again, we were always cool and I cared about her, but it was not love. As an only child, she was used to having her way. As the oldest of three children who grew up in my household, I was always the one who had to make the sacrifices. This may not be true, but it seems like the siblings who have to make the most sacrifices are the ones who are strong enough to endure the pressures in life.

People who have everything given to them cannot stand the first sight of adversity. When I asked for something and my mother told me no, I knew that meant "hell no." On the other hand, when Kelly's mother told her no, she would start to cry and would usually end up having her way.

How could I deal or compete with that? I decided that for the moment, I had to block this out of my mind if I was going to finish boot camp. My company commander was a Filipino, and just understanding what the fuck he was yelling all of the time was pressure enough. If I dared to correct him, he would get upset and start talking in his native language. For a moment, you thought you were in the foreign military, but our government had an agreement with the Philippines when we had a base in Manila. The agreement allowed for a certain number of Filipinos to join the United States Navy since we occupied their territory. The majority of personnel in the Navy in San Diego were of Filipino descent. My company commander was one mean SOB, though. He was only about 5 feet 5 inches and weighed about 140 pounds wet, with bricks in his pockets, but he was a yeller. For punishment, he sent me and others to a place called short tour to learn discipline and to stop moving around in ranks. Since I was going to be a father, that made me more focused to finish basic training.

Boot camp was only eight weeks long, and before you knew it, graduation day had come. That was a major milestone that I was very proud of because to date, I had not completed most things that I had started. Most of the black kids did not have parents who came for the graduation because the tickets were too expensive. I still had four months of schooling to complete before I was going to be allowed to go home. I had not told anyone about the pregnancy because I joined the military with a clean slate and I did not want anyone to have a reason to make things tougher on me than it already was. How would Uncle Sam feel about digging deeper into its pockets to help an uneducated black boy from the south who was going to have a bastard baby? My guess was that they would soon be rid of me than take that chance, so I kept the pregnancy to myself. Besides, the baby was not born yet, so there was no rush. Terri had been completely removed from the picture and I was determined not to have a child of my own grow up without a father like I had. It was now February of 1986, and in a month I was going to have a chance to go home. Of all of the people I was most anxious to see, it had to be my baby brother Tyrone.

Tyrone was only nine years old when I left, and I was the only father figure that he had ever known. I was the only man who had ever been there for him, and he took it the hardest when I left home. I sent him letters and an allowance to make sure the bond between us remained strong. After feeling that I had gotten back on level ground and being with Kelly was my destiny, things got a little more complicated when she told me that she was having twins instead of one child. This was a true test for me. I could either deal with it or jump off of the nearest bridge. Again, I thought I had already paid for the mistake that I made of having unprotected sex, but now I was going to double that effort with twins. That was confirmation to me that my childhood days were over and I had to learn to be a man in a hurry. Twins was not a surprise to me as this would make the twelfth set in the family. I had two aunts and cousins with twins everywhere. If you were in my family, twins was something that you grew accustomed to, you somewhat expected it.

After finishing school in San Diego, I decided to cash in my ticket and ride a bus home to South Carolina to save some money. After all, I was going to have twins, and every penny I could save for the birth of the babies could be used. I was a 19-year-old kid making another decision that I thought was the right one. Needless to say, it was a terrible decision. The bus trip would last three days as I was perched on the back seat of the Greyhound bus, drinking tequila and talking to an old white woman who was going to Dallas. Bags were not checked in those days, and I decided that I would travel with a bottle of tequila. I offered my newfound friend some, and before you knew it, she was drunk and laughing nonstop. I tried to contain her before we got thrown off of the bus, but she laughed, drank, laughed some more, and then passed out. The first day was easy as I got to view the beautiful sights around Texas and Phoenix, but once the second day started, I started to smell salmon and I knew that there was no fish on the bus. I needed a shower in a bad way but there was no way to get one unless I got off of the bus. How could I be so stupid as to think that I could take a bus trip from one coast to the other? I was stinky, constipated, and frustrated all at the same time, but just like everything else, I had to learn from this mistake and press on. That day in March 1986, I swore on my mother that that was the very last time I would ever step foot in another Greyhound bus station.

A six-hour Greyhound trip can easily take you 12 to 18 hours. Finally, I got to Beaufort's Greyhound bus station after three days and Kelly was there to pick me up.

She looked like she was carrying a couple of watermelons, and I really did not know how to greet her. I don't think that either one of us had plans to see each other again, but there we were, about to become parents. We both knew that we owed it to our children to at least give it a valiant effort. Though her mother had remarried, like me, she did not have any kind of relationship with her biological father. To my surprise, her mother had also purchased her a car. Wow, I thought, we were on our way.

The homecoming went very well as Kelly stayed with my mother and me. We made the decision to purchase wedding rings to get married. Again, I was asking myself what the fuck I was doing and was I really ready for this.

How did I think I was ready to be married to someone at the age of 19? She had just reached her 17th birthday. Hell no, I could not do this yet; things had to wait. In the meantime, I knew that I had to make an effort to be an upstanding father, but who did I have to learn from? What man did I ever see at least attempt to be a father? All the men that I had ever known were good at making babies, but after that, they felt that their jobs were done. Was this the kind of father I was going to be? Could Kelly and I make this work? Once my aunts Nell and Mae found out that I was thinking about getting married, they came to my mother's house to have a little chat with me. They too assured me that I was much to young to think about getting married and I was just not the only man in the world who had made this mistake. They mentioned that it was very important to be a good father but if I was not ready to get married, I should not do it for that reason alone. I knew they were right and I should wait at least until Kelly finished high school before thinking of marrying her.

On April 11, 1986 my twin daughters were born, and I was there to witness the entire event. The entire family was there as we saw two precious little girls being cleaned up and checked by the nurses. It was unbelievable to me that I was a father at 20 years old and even more unbelievable that we had produced such beautiful looking children. We agreed that we would be good parents and provide for our girls, but it did not take long before those plans went sour. Love in a relationship can conquer many adversities, but when two people are not in love, it is just a matter of time before the two of you want to kill each other. We had two strikes against us from the beginning. I had not yet gotten over Terri, and Kelly felt like her childhood had been taken away from her. Besides that, I had to report to my ship, and she was just a junior in high school. What was I suppose to do? Was I suppose to marry her, take her with me to Virginia, put her in high school, and find babysitters that I knew I could not afford? We were playing the part of great parents in the beginning and pretending to be a couple in love, but soon after the girls were born, I was leaving for my ship in Virginia and I was leaving alone.

CHAPTER 11
THE SHIP

My two beautiful girls were born and I tried to give them everything that I could, but when you are making about 600 dollars a month, it does not go very far, especially since I was still expected to help my mother. My ship was in Norfolk, Virginia and I did not know anything about it or what pier it was on. Though I had promised myself that I would never ever ride a Greyhound bus again, I found myself taking that trip from Beaufort, South Carolina to Norfolk.

The trip took about 14 hours, and again, I was sore as shit when I got off of that bus. I met a young lady on the bus who was very friendly and she was heading back to Norfolk also. She explained that her brother-in-law was in the Navy and when we got there, she would ask him to take me to my ship. Fortunately for me, he was at the station to pick her up and he gave me a ride to my ship. It was very awkward to say the least. Her brother-in-law brought his wife with him to pick her up and we both had luggage. He was driving a Chevy Chevette and we were packed in there like sardines. I was sitting behind him and he had the driver's seat in the pimp position. He was basically lying down while he was driving. Who was I to complain, though? The ride was free and he knew where he was going.

I thanked him after I got out of the car and moved around for about five minutes until the circulation came back to my legs. As I walked down the pier to the USS Canisteo, "AO-99", I could see a sailor on the quarterdeck shaking his head as I got closer. As if I was not scared enough, the shaking of the sailor's head did nothing for my confidence. I walked up the brow and asked his permission to come aboard the ship just like I was taught at boot camp. The young sailor took a long hard look at me and said, "Welcome to the worst fucking ship in the Navy." The way he looked in uniform, I could see why he believed that. As I settled in, I was very scared because of all the stories I had heard about people suddenly disappearing when the ship went out to sea. The Officer of the Deck welcomed me and ask where I was from. When I told him that I was from Beaufort, S.C., he immediately gave me the nickname of "Cornbread". Who was I to argue, I would be "Cornbread" if that kept people off of my ass.

It was easy to see that the crew was racially divided when it came to liberty and social gatherings. It was 1986, and though much progress had been made, racism was still very evident on Navy vessels. I tried not to associate myself with any groups until I got familiar with my surroundings, but when you are young and join an organization like the Navy, you don't have to pick a group—they pick you. This is when I met Mark, who would be one of my best friends for the next 20 years. Mark was older and had been in the Navy for about eight years. He provided a little stability when there was none to speak of. I now realize that the people in the military are just a product of society.

Basically, you have the people in the military from all walks of life. You have smart ones, dumb asses, crooks, paranoid ones, mean, and friendly people. We had people on the ship who were very religious, honest, educated, gambled, loan-sharked, sold drugs, used drugs, and some who stole everything that was not bolted down. Also, the ship was a very segregated place. Whites hung out with whites, blacks hung out with blacks, crooks hung out with crooks, and gays hung out with anyone who wanted to be with them. Mark, who was my boss, took me under his wing and invited me to his home where I met his wife Jane and could get a good meal. Mark did not have much family back home who came to visit from Alabama, but within our workplace, we all were very tight. To this day, Mark is still one of my very best friends because of his honesty, integrity, and a genuine love for all people. I spent my first three months on the ship being a steward. Though I had joined the Navy to be a radioman and I had already completed my training, everyone who reports to a ship and who are E-3 and below must first work in the ship's mess before they can work in their chosen job field. I started working in the Chief's mess as their personal breakfast chef. Every morning, I had to make eggs to order. I was fortunate because the Chiefs paid for my services whereas the general mess did not. I was also lucky because I did not have to work for the officers.

All of the regular cooks were either black or Filipino. In the 1980's most minorities were still treated like shit and given jobs as cooks or boatswain mates on U.S. naval vessels. I just went on about my business and did what I was told so I would not bring any unnecessary attention to myself. In a way, it was still like being in the south. I knew many of the guys who were doing drugs and I did not want to get mixed up with that crowd. I was always told that I should not join the Navy because of all of the prejudice and the gay people. It wasn't as if the people who were telling me about the military's prejudice had a top of the line job with racial equality, so I ignored it. It was as if they thought that they too were deserving of the minimum wages that they were receiving. You have met the type so many times. The type that knows so much about everything but has not experienced shit. The type that wants to knock everything you try to do because they have nothing going on for themselves. The type that can only see from one week to the next because he does not plan to be around for the long haul. How can you be treated like shit all day by your boss for minimum wage and tell me how prejudiced another organization is when you have never been a part of it?

After my three months was over from working with the cooks, it was time for me to go to my shop and become part of the communications team. Shortly after going to my workplace, my division was lobbying for someone to go to International Morse Code school. The school was in Charleston, South Carolina, and no one wanted to go there. This was a chance for me to go home and spend some time with my girls. Weeks passed and I headed back up to South Carolina to settle in. Also, this would be a perfect time for Kelly and me to get closer and see if we were going to be together as a couple. When I arrived in Charleston, Kelly could not come to pick me up, and my mother wasn't too happy that she had to come on short notice. In thinking that everyone would be elated because of my arrival, I did some soul searching and just downplayed what had happened. When I got to my mother's house, I phoned Kelly to tell her that I was home, but she had other plans and went out with her girlfriends. That is when I realized that I was not top priority on her list. At my mother's table on a Friday night, I grabbed a fifth of

Seagram's gin and commenced to drink until the bottle was empty. My mother was upset and was asking if I was just going to sit there and drink myself to death. No matter what Kelly and I did, we could not get along and it seemed like we were just heading in different directions. How could I blame her—she was about to be a senior in school and she had the rest of her life ahead of her. Though I don't think that we were in love, I was willing to make this work for the sake of our children. Terri was not in my life and she had gone in a different direction. Over and over again, Kelly and I just could not get it together. We were too young for marriage, and I could not envision her as part of my future. We met one Saturday night and decided that we did not want to be tied down with each other. Lord knows what would happen now. I had fallen into the statistical trap once again. I was a single father with two children, and that was nothing to be proud of. I wanted to be the best possible father I could, but the children already had two strikes against them, and they were Kelly and I.

Once I returned to the ship, they put my ass to work full throttle. The Navy figured that they had put me through a year's worth of school in my two years of service and they wanted a return on their investment. I was back in Norfolk, Virginia and to say that it was a party town is an understatement. I had no one to answer to. I had no woman who I wanted or wanted me. That was fine. I could just chill for a while and get my career together. It did not take long before I got my ass beaten on the ship. In the eighties, if you didn't do what you were told on a military ship, you were a prime candidate to get an ass whipping. They would not do it in the open because it was not permitted, but once the doors were locked, the sessions sometimes started with a slam to the deck. I knew that if I was to survive that ship, I was going to have to be smarter. I learned my job as a communicator quite well. My pay increased and I started making about 800 dollars a month, and I was giving Kelly and my mother a good portion of that, which left me broke on payday.

Since I could not get anyone to co-sign for an automobile for me, I ended up buying a Datsun 310 GX. The car was old, had about 90 thousand miles on it, and the air conditioner leaked on the inside. Besides that, I had some seat covers on it that let everyone know that you were riding in my car. Those were the first seat covers I had ever seen that shed fur. Through it all, it was my car that I bought on my own without anyone's help and I loved it. I might as well had been driving a Porsche. I learned at an early age that if you buy something with your own money, you will take better care of it and you will appreciate it more.

After a year went by, I managed to make the rank of a Petty Officer Third Class. Though that was only the rank of an E-4, you could have told me that I was an Admiral and I would have believed you. Many things would change with that position. First of all, that is one of the highest pay jumps on a Navy ship because I was now eligible for sea pay. My pay raise was more than 400 dollars a month. The way the money crunch was, that was a relief, and I knew that with the right planning, I could have some spending money in my pocket. It also came at a time when my car was on its last leg, as I did not trust to take it on I-95 anymore, so I did what every typical young black man does when he gets a pay raise—I bought a damn car. The money enabled me to buy a new car that had 12 miles on it. It was a 1987 Chevrolet Spectrum. My friend Mark joked that his lawn mower engine was bigger than the one in the Spectrum, but I did not care. It was new, and again, it was mine. With no credit history to speak of and no co-signer, I got the car at a whopping 21 percent APR. You know the signs, "We finance E-1 and above". In plain English, that meant that I would never ever pay off that damn car, and if I did, I would end up paying for it three times. I did not know what the future held, but I did know that I was riding and I was happy.

On a ship, there is always one guy who you cling to in a way that you know he has your back if things go wrong. On the USS Canisteo, it was a guy named Randy.

Randy and I became very good friends and we started hanging out together. Mark was my boss and a good friend, but Randy was right around my age. What made our relationship even better was the fact that he loved to play basketball and he did not smoke or drink. He too was an E-4, and he had received a big military bonus of 20 thousand dollars for re-enlisting. Of course, he did what most black men end up doing with that kind of money when he is not used to it. He bought a damn car. No investment, no CDs, no stocks, just buy the damn car and live for now. Randy ended up buying a Volkswagen Jetta and it was beautiful. We decided to take it on I-95 to test it out, and before we knew it, we were on our way to South Carolina. The military is like that—you could just be chilling one minute, and then the next minute you find yourself in New York City. When Randy and I got to my mother's house, he was treated like royalty and he made himself feel at home. I introduced him to my entire family and they loved him because he was funny. I also introduced him to Kelly and my daughters.

By this time, Kelly and I were still friends, and every now and then, we would talk about trying to make things work out between us. We did not spend too much time on that kind of talk because we both knew that, deep in our hearts, it was bullshit. With Randy, the trips back to Norfolk did not seem that long. He would joke most of the way, and it seemed like we were back on the ship in no time. After that trip, I decided that it would be a while before I went back to Beaufort. I had to find my niche and I could not do that if I was going home a couple times a month. I mean, what was the big deal of being away from home if I was going back there a couple times a month?

Being on my ship from 1985 to 1989 would really aid in my development as a man. When you join the military, you are in direct contact with people from all walks of life.

We had people from all parts of the United States with different backgrounds and different religious beliefs. I even had one guy named Dave who told me that he had not seen a black guy until he came in the Navy. Of course I thought that this was impossible, but he tried to convince me that it was true. Dave and I became good friends. He was mostly curious about me at first, but when he got to know me, he genuinely liked me. I was certain of this after he invited me to go home with him one weekend to Atlanta, Michigan. I had no idea where in the hell Atlanta, Michigan was, but after carefully thinking it over, I agreed to go up there with him. He warned me that people would stare because they would not be accustomed to seeing a black guy in that town, but he assured me that I would be safe. Dave and I decided to take one of the other guys from work who did not have anything to do. Wow, I was about to embark on a road trip with two white guys going across the country. That would have been unheard of where I was from, and I was sure that when we got to his house, the people there would think that he was out of his damn mind for bringing a person of color to their town. If my folks back in Beaufort had of witnessed that, they would have sworn that I must have been kidnapped.

The trip took us about ten hours from Norfolk because we had three drivers. I wanted to put that Spectrum on the road anyway, so it turned out nice. Once we got to Dave's house, his parents, sister, and brother greeted us and made me feel at home. I thought that they were treating me too well. It was one of those deals when someone is trying to overcompensate for something instead of being themselves. He took me around the neighborhood and everyone was just excellent. I know that they must have had an advanced warning that I was coming to town, but just like Dave said, I was definitely the only black person in town. The women found me to be very unique because I had a deep southern accent and was pretty confident of myself.

When one of them asked me if I wanted to go with her to get some pizza, I nicely declined. I am not that dumb to think that there would not be some asshole just waiting to start trouble for me. Dave was proof, though, that there are only two kinds of people in this world. There are good people and there are assholes. Color really does not have anything to do with that.

Dave's father took us hunting with a rifle and a bow and arrow. Deer were big in that part of the country and they made the best venison steaks I had ever tasted. For a split second while we were in the woods, I thought to myself that if they wanted to bury me, no one would ever know what the hell had happened to me and I would be a distant memory, but Dave and his family were one of the best experiences I had ever had. Where I was from, you did not see that kind of interaction between family members. You rarely saw a man in the house, and when you saw them, they were probably there to take a shower and hit the streets. We sat around the fire, and Dave's father told us stories as we drank beer and ate venison steaks.

When it was time to leave, I hugged the entire family, and they told me that I was always welcome back to their home. I am telling you, it was one of those Little House on the Prairie shit. They packed us a lunch on Sunday, and we were on the road heading back to Norfolk. As we started that long drive, I was reflecting on the weekend that I had just encountered and wondered how a man who had never really had any kind of relationship with another man of color accepted me that easily and got his family also to welcome me into their home. When I used to see a black man riding in a car with white guys, I used to think that he was such a sellout. Again, that was some bullshit we were taught to further help to imprison the mind. Just like a recipe, genuine friends come with many different ingredients.

As time passed, I met a young lady in Virginia that I thought could have had the makings of being my woman. She seemed smart, dressed well, and was pretty. Brenda had an innocence about her that really came out. She did not say much, but her eyes really told the story. I met her at a party that one of my shipmate's girlfriend was having. My friend Edward was a pretty good-looking guy, but his girlfriend, who he called Peaches, was not too pleasant on the eyes. She was over two hundred pounds and really did not have much going on in the looks department. When she smiled, she looked like Leon Spinks. I don't look at myself as being a shallow person, but I always thought that if I had to wake up and look at a woman like that every morning, I would rather just be shot in the head and get it over with quickly. I was wondering what in the world they could have in common, but it was soon revealed. Eddie was an alcoholic, and she was a lush. One of her attributes was the fact that she was a very good cook and she kept a very clean bathroom. I usually make it a habit to find a way to ask a woman to use her bathroom when I visit just in case she asks me to eat something. If a woman has a clean bathroom, she is usually clean, but if you walk in there and you see shit everywhere, you better say that you are not thirsty and that you are full. A woman who does not clean her toilet and bathtub probably does not clean her ass adequately, either. I decided to make the first move and talked to Brenda. She seemed a little nervous, but I could tell that she was very interested. My relationships never really had a chance to go anywhere because I still had my hang-ups over Terri. Terri was dating someone else, so I had to get over her and get on with my life.

CHAPTER 12
DATING

Now, this was definitely the time to sow my oats. I was not obligated to anyone but myself and I liked it that way. I knew that Kelly could never work and Terri was a distant memory that had passed. It was good for me to meet Brenda and possibly give love a chance. We did many things together and had many things in common. Before I knew it, I was meeting her parents. Her parents were divorced but remained good friends. One day, Brenda asked me to meet her at her father's house when she was getting off from work. I agreed and was to meet her late in the evening. I arrived at her father's house before she did and decided to knock on his door. When I told him who I was, he answered the door with a pistol in hand and said, "Oh shit, I thought you were someone else."

When Brenda arrived, I told her about it when her father stepped out. She confessed to me that her father was a loan shark and he probably thought I was someone else. I guess that should be expected when a man has a fancy car, fancy clothes, fine furniture, a nice home, and does not have a regular nine-to-five. That scared the living shit out of me because I knew now that if I pissed this girl off, her father could easily have my ass. Our relationship was somewhat sealed when I was in a club one day with some of my friends. We were all sitting at a table laughing with some girls when Brenda came in. All of a sudden, this non confrontational woman, who would not hurt a fly, walked into the club and started going to my ass physically. She was not letting up as she snatched my earring out of my ear and snatched my chain off of my neck.

The club manager kicked both of us out, and as I was trying to explain what had happened, it just made her more outraged. Of course I could not do anything except try to calm her down. This was the second time that I had ever got into a tango with a young lady, and both times, I ended up on the short end of the stick. During my senior year in high school, a friend of mine named Tonya did the same exact thing to me because my cousin was sleeping with her boyfriend. Again, I managed the same fate by being scratched like I was in a fight with a cat. This was not going to work. I was afraid of her father and I now saw another side of Brenda that I did not like. Shit, who knows, she just might have been mad enough to have her father put a hit out on me. It was time to move on and that is when I met Angela. Angela was pretty enough, but there was a major problem straight from the beginning. On our first date when I picked her up from her home, she forgot to mention the fact that she had three small children. I did the math and decided that I did not want to get involved with a 21-year-old woman who already had three children by three different men. Either she did not know birth control existed or she was dumb as hell. Either way, that was a lost cause from the beginning because I was not going to make kid number four. In the short span of five months, I met four woman with the name of Angela. That has to be the most popular name given to an African American female. It took me a while to figure it out, but many women in the Hampton Roads area of Virginia really could care less about how much money you made as long as you were in the military and they could get some benefits for little Johnny. A couple of weeks later, I met Sabrina. Sabrina was dark like me and had one child. I could deal with that, and she had her own apartment. We decided that we would get to know each other and just be friends before we both did something that we would regret. I agreed with that because she seemed to be levelheaded, with a college degree, and she knew where she was going in life.

After about two months, Sabrina asked me to stay at her house but assured me that she was not ready for sex or anything. She wanted me to stay at her house but reminded me that she wanted to take things slow. I thought that her reasons were legit and respectable. I could respect the fact that she just did not want to engage in sex. We decided that night to just sleep in the bed but not to engage in any kind of sexual activities. At about three in the morning, I felt a very warm and tingling sensation running down my leg and I knew that it was not pussy.

She was actually snoring and at the same time, pissing on me. This girl was in her early 20s and had a bed-wetting problem. She had a weak bladder that was enhanced when she was drinking. The wine must of knocked her out cold. When I called her name, Sabrina did not move, and there it was, a big piss stain right in the middle of the bed. Now, I don't care how good a woman looks—piss smells like piss. Believe me when I tell you that no one wants another person pissing on them. Nothing else needed to be said at that time. I mean, what in the hell was I going to say if she had woken up? "Why did you piss on me?" You pissed on me but I understand? I know you pissed on me but I still love you boo? Hell no! I just put my clothes on, with a big piss stain on them, and walked out of the house in amazement. As I was driving back to the ship, I was trying to think about what I was going to say once I reached the quarter deck. When I crossed the quarterdeck of the ship, the guy on watch said, "I smell piss" and asked me if I smelled it. It was about a 20 minute drive from Sabrina's house, so the piss had time to settle in and marinate. I shook my head to say no and headed straight for the showers. From that time on, the guy on the quarter deck looked at me funny every time he saw me.

Finally, I met Phyllis. Phyllis was a nurse who introduced herself to me. I was at a bar called the Fox Trap when she walked up to me and asked if I would dance with her because it was her birthday. I think she told me her entire life story during the five-minute dance. Phyllis had a son and wanted another baby. She was approaching 30 years of age and suggested that her time was running out to raise a family. She also stated that she did not want to be an old maid raising a child. I already had two kids whom I could not afford already, so how would I look trying to bring another child into this world? Of course, this was not going to work, and I ended that relationship before it started. A wise person once said, "There are millions of women in the world. What are the chances of meeting your soul mate the very first time?" At this point, I decided to take a step back and stop going to the bars and clubs.

You cannot look into a coal mine and hope to find diamonds. It just does not work that way. How was I going to find the ideal person for me if the only places I frequented were clubs and bars? How could I find a woman with the kind of values I was looking for in a club or bar? The chances of that happening were not in my favor. You cannot keep a woman at home who is used to partying all of the time. I did not go to the clubs and bars every week, but when I did, I saw the same females. I knew that they were not coming to the club because I was there, so that had to have meant that they were actually coming to the clubs every single week. As the saying goes, "You cannot turn a whore into a housewife." Also, Norfolk, Virginia is saturated with the military. A military base will bring in cash to a local community, but it will also bring in the weirdest people you would ever want to see.

Some folks are just meant to be single. It is something within them that they don't want to fully share themselves with others. Many of those people don't want to have children because they think that children will somehow hold them down. During the Christmas holiday of 1988, with nothing to stay for in Norfolk and wanting to see my daughters, I decided to go home to Beaufort. I had not been there in a few months and thought that it was time to give my family a visit. When I got home, it was the same as usual. People were very happy to see me, but of course I had to hear all about the problems everyone was having also. I loved to visit my people, but for some reason, my relatives thought that I had some money. I mean, they actually thought that on a E-4 military pay, I was raking in top dollar. It was worse when I went to my aunt Jackie's house. As soon as I walked through the door, she was asking me what I had brought back for her and how much money I had to give her. If I told her that I did not have any, she would try to entice me to go to the bank. When that did not work, the story came up about when she used to raise me when my mother would just take off, and all of the other things that she used to do for me in my mother's absence. If that was not enough, her children were no better. They would start to ask me for money or anything that they thought I had even before they would say hello. It got to the point where I just stopped going to my aunt's house altogether.

Many women raise their children as single mothers, and God bless them for doing that. In the African-American community, it is much more prevalent than it is in the white community. The job of raising children alone is tough, but we have to know that our children do not owe us for being born. They never asked to come into this crazy world, so to hold them hostage is just wrong. Many black young men cannot get off of the ground because they are too busy trying to take care of a wife and a parent. This leads to problems in relationships with other women because you have to understand young men that your mother is not a wife. I think that family should always help each other out and we should do all that we can for our parents economically, but the parents' job is to ensure that the child grows up to be a healthy adult that is able to take care of his or her children. When I hear a parent say something like "He could never pay me back!" I just want to scream. I want to say, "Pay you back for what?" He could never pay you back for not protecting yourself and getting pregnant before you were married?

Or, he could never pay you back for letting that guy who is already living at home with his parents get you pregnant. I am also not saying that black people are ignorant and whites are smart, because that is far from the truth. The last time I checked, though, I was black and we have too many issues for me to be talking about the problems that white people have.

During my time at home, I ran into an old classmate of mine named Carol. Carol had a very nice figure but she was nothing too pleasant on the eyes. What she lacked in the beauty department, she made up with a great personality. You will find some women that are absolutely gorgeous on the outside, but their personality immediately makes them unattractive. Then you will find someone like Carol who may not be the most beautiful girl, but her smarts, personality, and charm compensates for her looks. We greeted each other and she mentioned to me that Terri was home for the holidays. I told her that I wanted Terri to call me, but I never expected that to happen.

As I chilled at my mother's house, Terri phoned me that night and we had a very nice conversation. We had not talked at all since the birth of my twin girls, and I thought that we would never actually have a chance to talk again. Terri told me she was going to leave the next day and that I could visit her in Columbia. I would not leave immediately, but after sitting around for a couple of days, I decided to take the trip to Columbia to see if what Terri and I had could really be rekindled. She had a roommate named Maria who was very nice and did not have a problem with me staying there. I would find out later that Maria was not playing with a full deck and was actually a little crazy. The way I saw it, Terri was a little naïve because Maria was in love with her. That was one of the hidden agendas of Maria's that were not told. Terri had her own issues with a boyfriend named Daniel who was obviously used to coming over. By the second night, she just told him that I was there and that I was not leaving. I realized that she still had some feelings for me if she was willing to do that with our future being so uncertain. We really connected, and I realized at that time that she was the only one that satisfied me. It was a time of growth because after sex, a woman has to satisfy you emotionally or the relationship will never work.

She could joke around with the best of them, but she could also be very serious and witty when she wanted to. Terri was raised by and around many old people, and she just about had a saying for everything, like "A new broom may sweep clean, but the old broom gets the dirt" or something like "Watch the dog that brings the bone because he always has one to take back."

I also admired the fact that she was ambitious and was not just sitting on her ass watching soap operas and waiting for someone to do something for her. I was not going to fuck this up this time. I was going to act like a man and treat her like a woman. She did not have to say anything, but she was willing to accept me with my two girls. If she was not willing to do that, there would be no way that we would be able to get to first base. At the time, the children were not going to be in the picture much because Kelly and I had gotten to the point where we pretty much disliked each other. That was terrible for the children because they really did not deserve the kind of parents that we were. To her credit, though, at least she was there all of the time. Terri and I made a pact right then and there that we would be together and work any problems out that we may have. After that, there was absolutely no chance that I was going to be with a woman like Kelly, who I did not love anyway. So many times, people get married or stay together for the wrong reasons. No one wants kids to be without a parent in the household, but you also don't want kids to grow up with low self-esteem, insecurities, or hatred in their hearts by listening to parents argue and fight every night.

The ride back to Norfolk from Columbia seemed refreshing and smooth. I thought about my visit and how it was a total success. I also knew that I had the potential to be very successful if I was connected with the right woman.

CHAPTER 13
MARRIAGE

I was on one of my weekend passes and I decided to spend it with Terri. When I was with her, those weekends seemed to absolutely fly by. I would usually get there on a Friday evening, only to have to leave on Sunday.

That drive from Norfolk, Virginia was brutal on the body but that one full day seemed worth it. During my travels on I-95, many things would go through my mind. You can think about and do a lot of dumb shit on a six-hour commute. To shorten my time to Columbia, I would try only to stop for gas. I found myself needing to use the bathroom many times on the road before I was ready to stop, so I perfected pissing in a bottle while driving. I had to make sure that there were no trucks or SUVs around because the last thing you needed was someone calling the highway patrol because you have your Johnson in your hand while driving. Once cleared, I would fill the bottle, cap it, and dispose of it when I ran out of gas. If you think about it, though, the time I saved was minimal at best. I had to stop for gas anyway and it would have only taken me an additional three or four minutes to use the toilet. I would also do dumb shit like count the make of cars to see how many of that type were on the road. My worst habit was picking up hitchhikers. I knew that it was not a good practice, but I was bored and they provided some excitement during my travels. Once I picked up a guy who could hardly fit in my front seat. I was driving a Chevy Spectrum and he had to weigh just as much as the car. He was an insurance salesman who had ran out of gas. I was not worried about him; he was more worried that I was actually going to rob him than I was of him robbing me. Another time, I picked up a woman who was thrown out of a tractor trailer by a trucker. She said that they got in a argument and he put her out on the side of the road. She said that she would not put out, so the trucker told her that she was wasting his time and put her out right in the middle of the freeway. It has been my experience that truckers are the strangest people that I have ever met. I have never met a trucker with an IQ over ten. That woman should have known that if she had gotten in the truck with one of those guys, they were going to expect her to put out. I will put truckers and wrestling fans in the same weird pot. Have you ever gone to see a wrestling match like the WCW or WWF live? If you have ever done that, I know you had to be thinking about what the hell you were doing there?

She stayed awake for most of the commute and only dosed off to rest after she was convinced that I was not going to kill her. We all think we have problems, but how bad could that lady's problem could have been if she was willing to hitchhike from state to state? Of course I did not pick up just anyone. I never picked up those people who looked like they lived on the road or looked like instant killers. There was no way to tell the good ones from the bad ones, but I trusted my instinct and judgment to protect me.

Terri would always be happy to see me, and we would usually head on over to Captain Dee's to get some seafood. I cannot believe that we used to go to Captain Dee's that much because the thought of the place now turns my stomach.

Terri often asked me if I wanted to be married, but I did not think much about it until she told me that she needed more of a commitment from me. How could I blame her? I would be there one minute, and the next minute, I could be gone. She wanted to make sure that I was committed to the relationship this time. The only thing I had to ask myself was if I wanted to be with this woman for the rest of my life. My experiences with women told me that Terri was the absolute best thing that I had going for me. I still was not even sure about the military. As far as my pay went, I figured I could have made that much washing dishes somewhere. I had just made the rank of E-4 and it still did not leave me much after paying child support. At least I knew that she did not want to marry me for my money, because I was dead broke. Once I agreed to do it, she told me that I would have to ask her father for her hand in marriage. Oh boy, her father did not care too much for me. Terri's father knew my father and thought that there was no way I was going to marry his daughter. His daughter was in college and was going to do great things. Why would his daughter want to marry a young man in the Navy who already had two kids?

Her mother felt the same way and let it be known to all that I was not good enough to marry her daughter. My mother was not going to be too chummy about it either, because I was also giving her a small cut of my check. If I had a wife, there was not going to be a cut to give. So the only people who were going to be happy with the announcement of the marriage were Terri and I. When I got to her father's house and I explained to him that Terri and I wanted to get married, you could tell that he was disappointed and told us that he thought we were too young to get married. We were 23 years old, and he thought that we should wait a while to do it. I looked at it a different way. I figured that he wanted it delayed because he felt that if it was, I would find a way to fuck it up before we tied the knot. To my surprise, Terri told her dad that it was respectful for me to ask his permission, but it stopped there. She explained to her father that she wanted his blessing, but she did not need it and was going to marry me regardless of his wishes. I was impressed to see her stand up to him like that. Before we left, he gave his blessing, and I am sure he prayed very hard to God that night asking him to please give his daughter some sense not to marry me. Of course, he had known my father and grandfather as good-time men who loved to drink and chase pussy. He also knew that my father loved to brag about how he kicked women in the ass if they did not do what he wanted. Terri's father did not want that type of life for her, and who could blame him.

Next in line was my own mother. My mother liked Terri but she did not figure me on getting married yet. She had hinted that I set up an allotment for her with my military paycheck and I had not gotten around to that yet. Of course, if I was to get married, I surely would not do that now. Besides, I knew that Terri would be good for me. She could control me like no other woman. For some reason, I really cared about her feelings where I mostly did not care about other females. I was one of those men who thought that females always had an agenda, and no matter what happened, you were always going to come out on the short end of the stick when you dealt with them. My friend Mark who is like family has a favorite saying that goes, "Friends and family will fuck you every time." Terri was the first girlfriend of mine who would give me 20 dollars if she had 30. That genuine and sincere affection for me was about to have me do something that I thought I would never do, and that is to get married. Getting married was easy enough, but how would I be sure that I loved her enough to stay with her at the age of 23? How did I know that some sweet little thing would not cross my path and blow me away? I could not be sure that this would not happen. What I did know was that this was the first woman I had ever been involved with where sex was not the first thing that registered in my mind. That meant a lot to me, because any couple that gets married on the basis of sex or finance alone doesn't have a chance in hell of making the marriage last. Sooner or later, you must have something else in common besides good sex. A woman can have a body like a Mercedes-Benz, but if she is clueless, that man will eventually leave her. Most of us want someone who can think on her feet, know how to manage a bank account, know how to cook, and know what is going on in life besides the dumb shit that they see on television. The days of the Waltons and the Brady Bunch have passed, and men really don't want to deal with the women that we term "dead weight." That is the woman who sits at home all day and waits for the man to bring home a paycheck so she can buy a dress. Terri was as ambitious as I was and maybe even more. The only thing I wanted to change about her was to get her to stop wearing those granny underwear that the old folks called bloomers. When she had them on, it made me feel like I was in bed with her grandmother, but she quickly got the hint and started wearing undergarments that were more appealing.

We were not going to have a large wedding. We only invited the immediate family, which consisted of about ten people. It would be a small church wedding given by a local pastor, and I was going to wear my Navy white uniform. My best man would be a friend of mine in the Navy named Darren. We were the same age, worked together, and my brother was unavailable serving time at the Beaufort Marine Institute. I had thought about Ronald, but he was on leave and Darren had no problem making the trip. Mark never believed in coming to weddings and decided not to make the trip. I had a couple more of my friends from the Navy attend in their military uniforms and we were ready to go. Terri and I decided that we would pay for a small wedding and a couple of weeks later, put on a big shindig with a reception in our hometown. After the wedding, we decided that we would go to an amusement park called Carowinds in North Carolina for our honeymoon. We were really on a tight budget and we knew that just being together would more than make up for any kind of glamorous honeymoon. Two 23-year-olds were married who did not know shit about life, but we would soon learn many lessons that would both drive us apart and then make our relationship stronger. Three weeks later, we had a reception in a small town in Beaufort called Dale at the local elementary school.

My family came together, planned, and paid for the entire event. I did not even have to pay for a DJ who was my cousin "Kid Boogie". That is one great thing about black families—they know how to come together for events like this. Everyone will get together and decide what they are going to do and what they are going to bring. It seemed like everyone was there to wish us well. With my family's reputation, her family thought that she needed all of the luck that they could muster.

Terri's mother came with her family, and I was hoping that she would feel comfortable there. Her father was coming with his fiancée, who he had been with for almost 20 years.

Terri always thought that her father's fiancée was crazy for hanging around with him for that long with no commitment. Her mother was still very bitter about the divorce, and it had eaten her alive for years. Later on, Terri's mother explained to me that she was the babysitter for her ex-husband's fiancée. As she explained it, her ex-husband's fiancée was out with her husband while she kept her kids. Imagine babysitting someone's children while they are out with your husband. Wow, that would be enough to drive anyone crazy. Terri's father denied that this ever happened, but if you are a man, even if you are caught red handed, you will try to convince your significant other that it was not you or she must have had a spell on you. Of course, Terri did not take sides on that issue, but she was very cautious with her friends around me. In a nutshell, if she was not around, she made sure that her girlfriends were not around me. That in itself spoke volumes. One of her favorite phrases was "I grew up with my father and many uncles, so I know the shit that men do and what women are capable of doing." She would explain to me that she had to lie for her father to other women on several occasions, so not only would I have to deal with all of the shit that my father left on the table, but I would have to deal with the reputation of her father also. That meant that maybe she was contemplating locking my ass up and never letting me go anywhere.

As her father walked in, he was his natural colorful self, lighting up the room from one end to the other. His fiancée walked behind him like a proud woman displaying a prize. I felt sorry for her mother because it seemed as if she had to endure yet another slap in the face. Many eyes were on her to see how she was going to react to the situation. He was very much over her, but it was very evident that she was not over him. The reception was great and the food was even better. Of course, once the reception got going a little, everyone went to the dance floor and started what seems to be a tradition at all-black wedding receptions. Once the music started playing, the young, middle-aged, and old were on the floor at the same time doing the electric slide.

Today, there are at least five different versions of the electric slide, but in 1989 there was only one. The great thing about the electric slide is you don't have to know how to dance to do it. The moves are simple, and once you look at it two or three times, you will pick it up.

Another great thing about the slide is that you don't need a dance partner to do it. You may have been turned down all night for a dance, but when the electric slide comes on, you finally get your chance to groove. Black folks treat the electric slide like the National Anthem at a wedding reception or a club. When they hear the sound, they automatically get up and head for the dance floor. Most of my relatives were looking sharp. Some had their gold tooth shined up, with the jerry curl freshly done and the Pro-Line curl activator keeping it together. Of course, if you did not have the short pants set with the dress shoes and tube socks, you were considered out of touch. I found it very amusing, because in the four years that I had left home and seen another part of the world, Beaufort seemed so prehistoric.

Terri called it "the place that time had forgotten." As country as my people are, though, I still love them to death. That entire day, I was wondering if that was the woman that I would be with for the rest of my life, or was this like many other gatherings that would only be a short-term memory. I had known people who had financed an elaborate wedding, reception, and honeymoon, only to get divorced before they ever paid for it. If you are not rich, I don't understand that concept. I mean, why put yourself in debt before you even get married? I believe that if you keep it short and simple, you can save enough to do the elaborate things later on in the marriage, but if you go into the marriage in debt already, you are heading for trouble. Of course, many people were giving us advice on how to stay married and what not to do.

The only problem I had with it was the fact that they were divorced or separated themselves. Have you ever wondered why so many people who cannot for the life of them keep a man or woman want to always give you advice on how to make your relationship work? That is like a person on crack giving you advice and lectures on how not to get on drugs and the bad things that they could do to you. I still did not feel like Terri's parents really wanted me to be with their precious daughter, but at this point it didn't matter anymore. I had to concentrate on pleasing my mate and only my mate. Trying to please anyone else would surely give our relationship the added pressure that new couples just don't need. It was also bittersweet because Kelly did not want our daughters to have anything to do with what was going on with Terri and me. I cannot say that I blamed her.

I thought that she was wrong, but of course I always try to put myself in another person's shoes before I am convinced that I am right about anything. Also, I knew that I already had two children, and Terri was young, fertile, and ready to have children of her own. I was going to be a young man with a bunch of kids. I knew that I would have to struggle before I could live the way that I wanted to. Being a parent takes on added responsibilities. For me, it was about precedence. Instead of buying that pair of shoes that cost 50 dollars, I would settle for a pair that was 25 dollars. I would constantly look for sales when I had to purchase something for myself. I had two children and a wife to support.

Terri and I had a modest beginning. We lived in a one-bedroom see-through. A see-through is one of those apartments where you can see everything once you step inside. All you had to do was turn your head to the left and then turn it to the right and you would see the entire apartment. It was not much, but it was ours and she kept it immaculate. We could not afford a good vacuum cleaner, so she used a broom to clean the rug. If it was one thing I loved about her, it was how clean she was. It seemed like we lived on pork and beans or stewed pork chops and rice. Either she loved those two meals or she couldn't cook anything else. To me, though, it really didn't matter. Hell, we were newlyweds, and the last thing newlyweds think about is food. The only requirement she had for me was to buy a house before we had kids. Terri said that she did not want to have a child in an apartment.

She wanted to raise our children in a house like she was raised in. Boy, life as a married man. I knew that I was going to be tested every step of the way, and it makes it even harder when you are not even sure if you are going to be a good husband. Like everything else that was put in front of me, I was willing to do everything I could to make my marriage a success.

CHAPTER 14
DECISIONS

For the first 19 years of my life, things were rather simple. I just had to make sure that I looked out for myself and not fall in with the wrong crowd. Now I had to be smarter because I had a lot on my plate. My wife wanted my undivided attention. My focus was not only divided, it was split into four. I figured that I would give my wife, mother, and two daughters equal time, and you cannot do that if you want to be married long. Terri was much more mature than I was, and I was the only person that she was worried about. The bible says that one should forsake all others and cleave to your spouse, but I was not ready to forsake the rest of my family. In a sense, that must have meant that I was not truly ready to be married. For this reason, I always tell young people to wait before they get married. I stress to them to get an education and get their finances together before they embark on marriage. If she loves you, she will not go anywhere. We sometimes get married for the fear of losing someone and then put added stress on the relationship because of finances and other issues. I was sending money home to my mother, and child support home to my children. That did not leave much in my household, and I knew that something had to change. Not supporting my kids was never in question, but I had to cut someone short and it was going to be my mother. She would have to understand that I had a family of my own now and I could not continue to send money every month. The second thing was the night clubs. Terri had the clubs out of her system, but then again, it was never in her system. I still loved to go dancing and at least look at the women.

My theory was that there was nothing wrong with looking at the menu as long as you did not order anything to go. I would come home late, and that would drive Terri crazy. Married people need time away from each other I would imply, but nothing constructive was going to come out of that statement. I started making a conscious effort to limit my night club activities, and if I just had to go somewhere, I would take Terri with me. Of course, a man never brings sand to the beach, so I was not going to take her to a club, but there were other things that we could do besides going to a club, like having a nice dinner or going to the movies. What young men have to learn is that once you get married, your spouse can actually become your best friend.

Married couples who cannot laugh and enjoy each other usually will not last. Many people in the world get married for business reasons also. They figure that their lives would be much more enjoyable if all of their finances were taken care of. That is also bullshit. Those kinds of marriages or arrangements are no different than a business transaction and seldom ever work out successfully.

I had gotten orders to Charleston, South Carolina, and that would make life a little easier for me because I was closer to Terri. Terri and I were looking for a house because we were ready to start our family. This was 1991 and it did not take us long to find us a little cozy starter home.

Compared to the tiny apartment that we had just left, that 60 thousand-dollar home seemed like a mansion. It was one thousand square feet with three bedrooms and two baths. At 25 years old, I felt like I had hit the jackpot. We were moving right along with two new cars and a new house.

I always had a certain outlook on life when it came to race and religion. Both have changed tremendously over the years. This is another decision that I made just by personal experience and maturity. I grew up believing that people of different color really did not have much in common with each other. In the south where I grew up, I was taught to have a very narrow-minded way of thinking.

It meant that one should frown at interracial marriages and hang around your own people. The question is, though, what is considered your own people? After seeing how whites treated people of color in the past, you would think that we all would learn from it and stop the stereotypes. One day, my eyes were opened forever when it came to race relations. I was leaving work one day in Charleston and had to go home to meet Terri to close on the house. I left my car lights on all day and when I tried to start it, the battery was completely dead. An older black guy, who used to preach to me about coming to his church, had just bought a new Lincoln Town Car. I waved him down and asked for a jump. After explaining my problem to him, he advised me that he had just bought the car and did not want to risk anything happening to it by giving me a jump. You talk about being selfish. How can you ever preach to me when you put that much emphasis on something that is material.

Initially, I thought he was joking, but he was very serious and left me there. Five minutes later, a white guy driving a Monte Carlo SS came along and asked me if I needed a jump. The car was nice and he had no reservation about giving me a jump and hanging around until the battery was fully charged. To make sure the battery was fully charged, he had me shut the car off and turn it back on. If that episode did not teach me anything about people and race, nothing would. Right then and there, I promised myself that I would never give my kids any speeches about hanging out with your own people or any other black bullshit that I had learned over the years. I am a proud black man who is proud of my heritage. My teachings to my children would be to treat everyone the way you would want them to treat you, regardless of status, gender, race, or religion. As I have said before, the only people in this world are good ones and bad ones, regardless of race. Black people will shit on you just like the white ones, and white people will take care of you just like the black ones.

Another subject that usually rubs me the wrong way is religion. I have either lived in or visited at least 20 countries, and I have seen every religion, which includes Muslim, Christian, Catholic, and everything else in between. Have you ever talked to a fanatic who thinks that just because you don't think like they do or subscribe to the religion that they subscribe to, you are destined for hell? Most of the people who I have witnessed like that are Christians. They believe that if you don't pray to a blond-haired, blue-eyed Jesus, you are destined to go to hell. Of course, that means that everyone who believes in another religion, which is most of the world, will go to hell. You tell them this, and they think that you are just absolutely out of your mind. It is also surprising to me how many black people actually believe that, since a religion like Baptist is really a religion received from the slave master.

Believe it or not, some people don't have a chance to pray to any religion. They are good people, but faith was never introduced into their lives. Then you have the people who believe that being good one day a week will get them a special invitation to heaven. They will put ten dollars on a church plate, but won't give a hungry person on the streets a dollar to buy a loaf of bread or won't let your ass change lanes when you are driving in traffic.

Have you ever seen the people who catch the holy ghost conveniently? It seems like they have to be in the mood and someone has to be around to cushion their fall before they catch it. Again, I don't condemn any religion; no one has the right to tell someone else how to pray and who to pray to. With that, I usually tell people that I am nondenominational because I know there is a God, but I don't believe he speaks to many of the people who claim he does. Finally, many people use religion to pray on the weak-minded and to gain wealth for themselves. No one should obtain wealth for delivering a message that he or she believes is true in their heart.

It took a while, but I knew that if my wife and I were going to make it, we would have to move away from our families. I was stationed in South Carolina, but the reason I joined the military in the first place was to leave the state. I was not next door to my family, but I was close enough to still be a part of their daily lives. If you want to get divorced quick when you are a young couple, all you have to do is live near one of the couple's parents.

Any problems that you and your spouse may encounter will surely be answered by your parents. It makes you wonder: if they really knew so damn much, how come none of them managed to stay married. We needed to be away, but that was not going to happen yet because I had a few more years left in Charleston.

On a cold December day in 1994, I received a call from a family friend named Rona. She informed me that Terri was about to go into labor with our second child. Our son Christian was scheduled to be born on Christmas, but I guess he got bored inside the womb and decided that he would make an early appearance. I got to the hospital just in time as Terri was about to go into labor. Everyone will always say it, but there is absolutely nothing beautiful about a woman going into labor. I don't care how fine you think she is. Once the doctors put Terri's legs in those stirrups and had her push, everything was coming out. When I say everything, I mean the baby, shit, piss, and everything else came out at the same time. Terri has a slender build and it seemed like the baby just popped out.

I think that she was in labor with our two kids for a total of ten minutes. Small women seem like they don't have much of a problem popping out babies, but fat women always have to get cut. Terri did not even have to be stitched up. I remember as a kid, when a woman went into labor in the hospital, they would stay in there for about a week.

Today, once you have a baby, the doctors are sending you home in 24 hours. Some women don't mind because hospitals will charge your ass 30 dollars for a pill. Uncle Sam has its fucked up points, but one of the benefits is that you can have a child and not come out of pocket for a red cent. Now that Terri had two children, I knew that my days of having more kids was over. Terri had two, but I had four and that was enough. I was thinking about how I could have all of my children under one roof and live happily ever after, but don't fool yourself because it just does not work like that. In your mind, you will tell yourself that all of your children will be treated equally. That could be true if all of them were in the same household, but there is no way in hell you can treat kids equally when you cannot spend equal time with all of them. When you have outside children, someone has to lose, and it is usually the children that is not in the household. The only comfort available to you is knowing that you are doing the very best for all parties concerned.

At that time, we decided that she would have her tubes tied while the doctor was already in there. Men always ask the woman if they would prefer a vasectomy. We ask that question knowing damn well that the woman will most likely say no. Men have a problem with anyone messing with their nuts, but sometimes it is not a bad idea just in case you plan to go dipping elsewhere. After watching two kids with heads as big as basketballs come out of that, I was in no rush to have sex. That had to be the furthest thing from my mind. My immediate concern was how I was going to take care of four children. Let's face it, I was not making enough to take care of everyone, and the pressure was starting to build. The only thing that kept me focused and aboveground was the fact that Terri did not put money ahead of love. She knew that with a base starting with love, all challenges could be met head on, and it wasn't like I was just sitting on my black ass—I was trying to do all I could to bring extra money into the household. We also knew that relatives were going to give us minimal support. Financially, we were going to have to fend for ourselves.

Marriage was great, but the military would be our toughest test. When we were together, everything seemed perfect, but when we were not together, it seemed as if I would end up in places that a married man should not be.

Part of that comes along with not finding new friends and hanging on to the old ones. You see, when you are married, you cannot do the same things you used to do, go to the same places you used to go, and hang out with some of the same people you used to hang out with. A rule of thumb to follow is that if your friend does not respect the fact that you are married, he surely does not respect you or your spouse.

Maybe it was immaturity or just lessons that had to be learned, but every time Terri and I took a step backwards, it was totally my fault. Somehow, I had gotten distracted and not realized what was really important in my life.

Somehow, I would end up drinking somewhere at a wild party and happen to be left there with a couple of my friends and the perfect number of women. Once you put yourself in that situation as a young man, there is no way to get out of it without alienating yourself. The men in my family were womanizers from the time I had ever known what a man was, and I did not know if I could be any different. One thing I will tell men is this: if you fool around on your spouse one time, it becomes easier to do each additional time. I have never used crack cocaine, but I would bet that it is somewhat of the same addiction. Your conscience plays with you at first, but it can quickly get to the point where you don't even think about it. I did not want to approach that kind of thinking, and I knew that it would not be fair to Terri. One thing that I did not have to worry about was a woman who was going to run around on me, so I considered myself lucky. Terri and I had survived my being stationed in Virginia. She had even decided to join me there for three years, and that is when our little successes started to form. She became a Delta and I became a Mason in the same year. With that, we had new friends. We had mature people who wanted to do more than party and go to clubs.

These people wanted to go to church, take kids fishing, hold job fairs, and get together at family functions. That was exactly what I needed, as the older mature men helped me to grow, put family first, and appreciated the black women for the queens that they are. Masonry taught me the balance of life and not to extend myself beyond my capabilities. It taught me that I should never ever judge a man for what he appears to be, but he needed to be judged for the kind of person that he showed he could be. Once I committed myself to a different lifestyle and friends, it was very easy to leave the night life and the binge drinking alone. I was finally feeling like I was growing up.

Masonry taught me that the mind and the body will only prosper from what you put in it, not from what people take from it. I found myself coaching Little League baseball and basketball teams and running a boys and girls summer youth camp. The pay was zero, but the appreciation one can get from nurturing young kids and being a role model is worth more than all the money in the world.

CHAPTER 15
POLITICS

It was now June 2002, and Terri and I had decided that it was time to leave Virginia and move the family back to South Carolina. I had gotten orders to Bahrain, which is a small Arabic country off of the coast of Saudi Arabia. I was to report there in September 2002 and all of my friends who were in the military were going to Bahrain, Kuwait, Saudi Arabia, or somewhere in the general area.

Something was going on, but we all were told that we were going there to show force in the region because Iraq had failed yet again to let the weapons inspectors complete their jobs and look for weapons of mass destruction. Well, it was not too hard to figure out that the build up of Military force had something to do with the events of 9/11, but why was everyone focused on Iraq when most of the men on the plane was actually from Saudi Arabia? I would have a specific job in Bahrain, but first I had to go to school in Georgia. I moved the family back into our house, which we had rented out for the past three years. The house that we had bought 12 years earlier looked like a wreck. It was a lesson to be learned as there is with everything that happens to you. The great lesson was to never rent out your house if you plan to settle back in it. No one will take care of your property like you will.

Another lesson was to make sure that you never involve personal relationships with business. The realtor that my wife and I used was a personal friend of one of my wife's best friends named Rona. Instead of using someone like Century 21 or Remax, we decided to give the poor old black business a chance to make some money. That was one of the damn worst mistakes I ever made. Business is business and bullshit is bullshit. Not only were they bad, I don't think that they ever went to the house to check on anything while we were away. In the contract, it was stated that no pets were to live in the home; however, we found out later that a German shepherd was living in the home. After spending about 5,000 dollars just to make the house livable again, we realized that it wasn't worth renting the house out in the first place. The only satisfaction that we received was the fact that we had a chance to be a traditional family, which gave both of us a chance to deal with family issues together instead of letting her deal with them alone. Once we moved back, my time home was going to be short-lived, as I, along with almost every military person that I knew, had orders to the Middle East to prepare for what eventually would be a war against Iraq.

After 9/11 happened, the focus was to protect America from terrorism. The military was told with certainty that Osama bin Laden was the mastermind behind the worst terrorist act to ever hit this country. We believed that, but much of the focus was being given to Saddam Hussein and Iraq. What we were focusing on was the buildup of Weapons of Mass Destruction and Saddam not being in compliance with orders given to let United Nations inspectors search the country for the WMDs.

Much was said that if we did not act to stop Saddam from completing his weapons, we might pay in a form of a mushroom cloud in a major city. Most people think that military men are just robots and we don't have the ability to think on our own. The truth of the matter is that every military man takes an oath to defend the country from all enemies foreign and domestic and to obey the orders of all senior personnel appointed over them, which includes the Commander in Chief. So, it really does not matter if you agree with the policies of the government; you still must perform your duties in a professional military manner. To say it mildly, the worst thing I think you could call me is a politician, because if you have a particular party that is winning an election with 53 or 54 percent of the votes, that means that approximately half of the people one way or another are basically believing a lie. What makes the United States the best country in the world is the fact that you can voice your resentments with a vote without any reprisals.

You can disagree with the President's initiative and still do your job professionally. If it were not like that, it would be impossible to win wars or to be the strongest military in the world. What also eats me alive is the fact that people call themselves Republicans and Democrats, or liberals and conservatives. I mean, what the hell is that? The person running for office is either right or wrong. I don't give a damn about belonging to a particular party.

I will vote for the man every time that I think is telling me the truth or at least is being more truthful in what he is saying. If two men are running for office and they are telling you something totally different, one of them has to be a fucking liar. You don't need a doctorate to figure that out. Then, once a politician is associated with that particular party, they are going to agree with them no matter what the agenda is. In saying that, it means that politicians don't run the country on the faith of what they believe; most of them run the country on what a particular party agrees to at that certain point and time. So when a person asks me what party I belong to, I tell them that I am an Independent. America is the strongest country in the world, but it also has some of the weakest people in the world. People let folks like Rush Limbaugh and Bill O'Reilly tell them how they should live, how they should dress, who they should vote for, and what is appropriate to say. You see these signs like "Rush is Right," or people wearing shirts like "The Factor," or bumper stickers on their cars, and you are like, get a fucking life. Those kind of people are getting rich because of the inability of middle-class America to be independent thinkers, and yet when people like Jessie Jackson or Al Sharpton speaks out on issues or gets paid for their services, America cries foul. If that is not some of the most flagrant bullshit that I have ever seen, I don't know what is.

Tavis Smiley, a great young speaker in his own right, got fired from BET for speaking his mind. You cannot tell me that this man poses any kind of threat to society, but when he tries to educate the African-American community on social issues, he is muzzled. BET basically tried to censor him because he will call a rat a rat. Oprah approaches these issues differently, but she is effective in her own way by giving so much to so many people. She should be commended for accepting the job as a role model, not only for African-American women, but for women of all races, backgrounds, and religions. When you think about it, she is really an activist in her own right. To me, she is the Rosa Parks of this generation because we only see the glamorous parts but we don't see all that she has had to go through to get where she is today. The ultimate for me will always be to someday meet Maya Angelo. I never wanted to meet superstar athletes or movie stars, but to me Maya Angelo is one of the greatest people to have ever graced the earth.

I have been in the military for over 20 years, and I certainly know that as long as you are in a position to kiss the right ass, the sky is the limit. It does not matter if you are in the military, a GS employee, or a cashier at Wal-Mart. Kiss the right ass, and you will go places. The bad part of that is when you have an employer that kisses his boss' ass. He then expects you to follow suit and do the same. In that sense, the military is no different than the civilian sector. Have you ever wondered how that person who started in the corporation a couple of years after you did, all of a sudden is now ahead of you or is actually your supervisor? Well, if you don't go to those corporate parties or laugh every time your boss tells one of those Godforsaken corny ass jokes, you better get with the program or you will be coming up from the bottom forever. I have the utmost respect for people who try to make it on their own merits, and as a person in a leadership position, the worst thing you can do for me is to kiss my ass. I don't like it because it does not come across as being sincere. You better believe that the same person that is kissing your butt is talking about you every chance they get. Earn their respect for being honest and having integrity, not for just being in a position that a degree or another ass-kisser has put you in.

I arrived in the Middle East and started executing my orders. The heat was nothing like I had ever experienced in my life. I was going to be there for a year, and initially, I was not certain that I was going to make it.

The base was small and very crowded. The influx of military personnel was huge, and almost every United States Navy ship was in the arena. Nothing was decided yet as far as declaring war, but everyone who was an independent thinker knew that we were going to invade Iraq sooner or later. Again, you would like to believe that everything that you were hearing was true, but this was politics, and politicians will say just about anything. The military's job is to execute, not to try and weed out the bullshit from reality, so we listened and waited for the next assigned task. If Saddam had a chance to do this all over again, I am sure that he would have chosen a different route. Not in his wildest dreams did Saddam think that we would actually invade Iraq. He played poker, and the President of the United States called his bluff. Not only did the President want to democratize Iraq, but many of us thought that this was also a personal vendetta. How would the President's legacy be remembered if he could topple one of the most hated men in the world and, at the same time, control one of the world's most oil-enriched countries? He would of gone down as one of the greatest Presidents in history if he could pull that off and control one of the world's most enriched oil countries.

I lived in a modest house in the Middle East where thousands of Americans and civilians from all of the armed forces had settled. The first thing I noticed about the people who lived in the Middle East was that it did not seem to have a middle class. When you looked around, the people were either wealthy or poor, but not middle ground. I was able to make a friend there who took me to the mosque and taught me a little about the Koran. It was amazing to me to see how much those people would pray daily. The prayer was done many times a day and you could set your watch by it. My Muslim friend's name was Jabil, and I asked him how he could go to the mosque eight times a day to pray. He looked at me for a second and asked me a question. He said, "If someone told you to show up at a certain location eight times a day, and for every time you showed up, you would receive a million dollars, would you show up?" I answered yes and he explained to me that true Muslims believe that they are receiving much more than a million dollars each time they pray to Allah. Of course I could not tell him the extent of why I was living in the Middle East or give him any information about the base. He respected that, and we became good friends.

As the days led up to the war, everyone was working 14 to 16 hours a day with no time for anything else.

Many ships were in the region and they depended on the people in Bahrain for logistical purposes. The weeks seemed like days because there were no such thing as weekends. We often lost track of what day it actually was. The work week in the Middle East was from Sunday to Thursday, with Friday and Saturday being their holiday time. On Thursday evening, you could tell that the weekend had begun because of the influx of the nearby Saudi Arabians. In Saudi Arabia, alcohol is not allowed, prostitution is not allowed, and women are not even allowed to drive. With all of that, the Saudis would hit Bahrain on Thursday evening and pretty much do anything that they wanted to do. Though they pretty much tore the damn place up, they were welcomed because they helped the economy.

Bahrain had all of the sex slaves who worked in the bars. These women were under contract by men from Bahrain who sold their services for a huge profit. The women of different nationalities included Ethiopians, Filipinos, Russians, Indians, Moroccans, and many other countries. To think, the military was using Bahrain to stage a war against Iraq, but as a country, it was a gigantic, manmade whorehouse with extortion of human rights. The women and men who were there from other countries to make an honest living were subject to insulting wages, making on the average of $100 a month. On the other side of that, the country was charging military personnel an average of $2000 a month to rent a villa or an apartment, which they called flats. The only people who had the houses to rent were already rich, so we were in essence making the rich even richer and thus aiding them with their purchase of more sex slaves and workers. It made me sick to see how many of the poor people were treated. Many African males were there also, and I would see them being kicked or even slapped in the face if their sponsor thought that they had done something wrong. The same guys who were handing out those kinds of punishments were acting like the Americans were their best friends. Since we had money and were paying up to four times more to live in some of the same places that the natives were living in, the business people in Bahrain treated us well. That did not fool me for a second because I knew that if I was poor, they would have probably been kicking my black ass also. When I saw that kind of treatment, it often made me wonder about life.

Because many Americans have so much luxury, will this be the only heaven that we see? Also, because those people were so poor, did not have decent clothes, shoes, and terrible hygiene, was this the only hell that they would encounter, and would they automatically be given the golden key to heaven? Were these people actually struggling the same way that Jesus did? I did not have the answer to that, but I believe that no man will struggle forever and no man can possibly prosper forever if he is not willing to share some of his prosperity.

I met several people in Bahrain who were just as homesick as I was. A civilian named Rova was in her forties, and she was a very wise woman. She was also married to a man who lived in Virginia, and she came to Bahrain like the rest of us to support the mission. We became good friends as she would shop for her husband and give me advice on items to purchase for my wife. What I loved about Rova is the fact that she was smart. She seemed to always be a cut above the rest. She was the best dresser in the arena and since most of the

Americans there were dawning a military uniform, she stuck out in the crowd. If there was a problem, she could solve it with her wisdom and always assured you that things would be just fine. During a time when a good meal was at a premium and friends were very scarce, she provided those things for some of us who needed it most. Another person who gave great support and advice was Queen, who was a Lieutenant Commander and was there with her husband. She was from Charleston, South Carolina, which is only about 60 miles north of my hometown of Beaufort. We all found that we had a lot in common and gave each other support. She would give people advice at every turn. I had a few male friends there who I could confide in, but most of the time, we worked our asses off.

The admiral called a meeting one day before the war and told us that in a few hours, Baghdad would be lit up like a Christmas tree and he appreciated the efforts put forth to prepare us for this most historic event. The president had given Saddam Hussein and his sons 48 hours to leave Iraq or be confronted with military action. At first, many wondered if it was legal to order a president to leave his own country. Don't get me wrong, Saddam Hussein is one of the biggest assholes known to man, and the world is a better place without him leading a country. With that said, I can think of at least ten other dictators that should be gotten rid of and the world would be better off without. Again, one thing is true about the military that is different from any other organization. Your job as a military person is to execute the plan, not try to figure out who is innocent or guilty. Every man and woman in the military contributed in some way when the takeover of Baghdad began. As we sat a few hundred miles away and gave the ships in the Gulf the order to execute, I could not help but to think about how many innocent lives were going to be taken. This is what the military calls collateral damage. Though we are much better at hitting the target that we aim at, it is still not a perfect system and innocent people would die. I started to think about the towers in New York City and 911, but I was not positive that we had the right man. I also knew that missiles did not have eyes, and there were going to be innocent women and children who were going to be killed. I did not give the order to go into combat against Iraq, but I was part of the system that executed the order. I wondered how the Muslim community would react to such an attack on Middle East soil. I got my answer the next evening as I caught a cab to my flat from work. Most of the people in Bahrain were not upset with the attempt to dethrone Saddam, but they pleaded that the women and children who were going to be killed were innocent. This was going to be quick and decisive. It was going to be over before anyone knew what happened. Iraq did not have the firepower to contend with us, and we knew it. We were certain that the war itself would last only about one to three months tops, and people would start to think about other things with Saddam Hussein now out of the way. We would be greeted as liberators. You talk about executing the wrong plan for the wrong war—we had it wrong. Three years later, Iraq is a hotbed, with insurgents killing the military and innocent civilians daily. You cannot save people who don't want to be saved.

You cannot democratize a country that wants to be a dictatorship. There has been no sighting of Weapons of Mass Destruction. Nothing has been found to suggest that America could have been attacked in the form of a mushroom cloud. Where was the smoking gun? Where is Osama bin Laden? Are the scare tactics about our national security we receive every couple of months legit, or are they used to mislead Americans into thinking that conservatives can protect the country better than liberals? With all of this, politicians can still tell the American people anything, and we are gullible enough to believe it. The world is supposed to be a safer place.

When I joined the military in September of 1985, you could put on your dress uniform, pull into any city or country around the world, and walk around town with your head held high, with nothing or no one to fear. The ships would pull into the downtown harbors and sometimes even be treated to the music of a local band upon arrival. Today, I would not dare put on my uniform in a foreign country because of the dangers that exist, and ships must have a secure port to pull into before they are authorized to do so. You don't have to be directly associated with the war to be a target—all you have to do is don the uniform. In my opinion, the world is not a safer place. You would do yourself a disservice to tell anyone outside the United States that you are a military member, without fear that they would try to plot something against you. You ask yourself, how can people hate others that much just because you are from a different place, but when you think about it, it is easy to understand. How could whites hate African-Americans and Indians so much in the early years of this country that they would enslave and poison them? If you can understand that, you will be able to understand why many around the world hate Americans so much. It can easily be said that the good we do actually outweighs the bad.

When the world is in a crisis, the United States military is usually at the forefront to deliver aid and goods. We have helped many countries when other countries like France have been slow to react. The smartest military men that I know are men like General Schwarzkopf and Tommy Franks. We go into the war, they get most of the credit for kicking ass, and then they retire and get rich selling books and making special guest appearances.

If you read this book ten years from now, you will find that we will still be occupying Iraq. You will find that we will still have a contingency there. Yes, Iraq is a mess right now, but if you don't know, it is also a gold mine if we are ever allowed to pump some of that oil for profit. When soldiers, sailors, airmen, and marines are asked their thoughts about Iraq, you are only going to get answers from the ones who have either been coached or influenced to say what is deemed politically correct. For the others, they have a voice, but for the so-called best interest of the military, it will never be heard. These men and women are honorable because everyone is willing to risk their lives for the safety of our country. We all may not agree that Iraq should have been invaded, but if you don a military uniform, you are obligated to support the mission, bottom line.

CHAPTER 16
CLASS REUNION

As the years pass, most are very intrigued about meeting again every decade or so. My high school class of 1985 graduated in the neighborhood of about 250 people, and many of us went on to be successful. When I measure success, I don't measure it by money alone. I look at the ability to be a good parent, be financially stable, and also be able to make a contribution to society and your community. You would be very surprised how many children actually need positive role models in the community.

Our 20th year class reunion was going to be at Battery Creek High School, and Edward, who was the class president, was organizing the event with the help of staff members. This event was being tried again, because at the ten-year mark, the money was given to a staff member named Sheila who conveniently lost it or should I say, stole it.. After that mess, most of the class was apprehensive about trying this again. It did not take long before the class president decided that he had too much on his plate and stopped participating with the planning of the class reunion. He was going through a messy divorce and had moved back home with his mother, so the class reunion was the last thing on his mind. This was his second marriage, and for the life of me, I don't know why when people get divorced, they feel that they have to go down that road again. It is as if they need a spouse to validate who they are. The task of planning the class reunion was taken over by four women named Constance, Sally, Joan, and Tabitha. They had the dubious task of planning a three-day weekend with events, and the hardest part of all was collecting the money. I was only in contact with Sally, and she was keeping me abreast of the progress. She was telling me about all of the people who were complaining and the checks she was receiving that had bounced. Now, at 38 years old and out of high school for 20 years, if you cannot come up with an honest 100 dollars for an event like this, you have not made many wise decisions in your life. I also knew that one of my best friends in school named Marion was not going to come because he had just been fired for stealing money from his job. All of the people who were not looking very pleasant also were not expected to attend. Sally was a good choice to head the committee because she was smart and aggressive. She and I had a very good bond except when as I mentioned earlier, she kicked my ass during a fight in high school. Her respect for me was at an all time high for the simple reason that I could of killed her, yet I refused to retaliate during the fight because she was a young lady. Sally could be hard when she had to be, and I knew that because even at a young age, she was a leader and not a follower.

Back then, Marion and I were close friends, and he was dating Sally. The only problem was that Marion also had an eye for one of my cousins. Sally approached me in the hallway at school and warned me about my cousin talking to her boyfriend. When I ignored her and just laughed, she pounced on me like a cat jumps on a mouse. I was always taught that a man should never hit a woman, and I carry that with me today. Sally knew this and when she was finished with me, I looked like I had been sliced by a butcher. I attended my wife's ten-year class reunion, and one thing that I learned from that one and all of the others that I had heard about is that most of the people who actually live in the town won't attend. Most of the individuals who do attend come from many different states and countries, but the people who only have to drive ten to 20 miles won't show up. It is as if they are embarrassed because they have never been anywhere, they feel that they are too fat, they have too many children, or they are just flat-out bums who have already been rejected by society and never actually got the memo that there is going to be a class reunion. You would be surprised how many people actually don't have an e-mail account, checking account, telephone, or many other necessities that are not required but make living in the 21st century a lot more pleasant.

I was in Indonesia and Papua New Guinea, contributing to the relief aid for displaced citizens who were devastated from recent earthquakes and the tsunami. With all of the current events going on, I was very uncertain if I would be able to attend the class reunion. Again, the United States was there giving aid to people who could not help themselves, and I don't care how long you live, there is no better feeling than helping people who don't have anything. I have been on both sides of the wall, and I will tell you that it is much better contributing to save a life rather than take one, like it was in the Middle East. As Sally kept me abreast of everything that was going on, I finally found out six weeks before the reunion that I was going to be able to come. I had not seen many of my classmates for 20 years, and it was indeed going to be a treat to meet some of my old friends who I played basketball with, skipped school with, and went to the nightclubs with. It was also going to be interesting to see some of the girls who I had a crush on in elementary school when I used to write little notes on pieces of paper to Debra that said, "Do you want to go with me, "yes or no." It was going to be great to see Londa who use to bring me grape Now and Laters to school every day. I was looking forward to seeing Erick to reminisce about the great basketball seasons that we had. My friend Mike would be there and we would talk about the good old days when we visited each other as kids and his grandfather would drive us around town going well under the speed limit at 10 miles an hour.

I got back to Guam from Indonesia and packed my bags to go home. I was not looking forward to that 18-hour flight back to South Carolina. Every time I took that trip, it felt as if someone had folded me up and put me in a suitcase.

Also, with my luck, I always ended up next to someone who just talked too much or a baby crying for the duration of the flight. Have you ever met those people who could just sleep through anything? I mean, if they had a piece of nail up their ass, they would still be snoring. The only way that I can drift off in a good sleep is if I am lying down in a comfortable bed and warm. I must also be clean before I can dose off in a deep sleep. If I don't wash, I start to itch automatically. Some folks can go to bed and sleep well after working all day long and only wash their body in the morning. If I don't wash before I go to bed, it feels as if my balls are on fire. The last thing a woman wants from a man is for him to be broke, but if you are broke and nasty, you will probably live a lonely life.

When my flight landed, I met my wife and two boys at the airport, who ran up and greeted me. My wife as usual did not eat while I was away and looked like she was about 100 pounds soaking wet. She was changing her mind back and forth about attending the class reunion because she said that she did not want to sit there and witness how many women I had actually slept with during my high school days. No one knew this, but like I told her before, my sexual activities in high school were very much grossly exaggerated. I could count on one hand of all the women that I actually slept with in high school, but since I had the reputation of being a jock back then, I never disputed what people were saying. Plus, one of my best friends Trevor would fuck a cat if given the chance, and I tend to believe that some of the stories about me were fabricated because I was associated with him.

Once I was settled at home for a few days and Terri and I had gotten reacquainted, I had to concentrate on moving my family into a new home before I started preparing for the class reunion. Terri was still undecided, and at this point, I didn't want to discuss it again because I felt that my class reunion was not about her. I wanted her to come with me and have a good time, but if it was going to be a problem because of tensions and dislikes, I would have preferred she not come. One of the females that I kept in touch with through e-mail just a couple of years earlier was going to be there, and Terri's dislike for her was tremendous. Of course, we were not seeing each other and we were not planning on doing anything, but some women feel that e-mails are a sign of cheating even though nothing in the e-mail had suggested it. It also does not help if your wife thinks that you actually fucked her in high school. Again, though, my reputation exceeded what I actually accomplished with women. I always say, if you are a woman and you have the man, why worry about what he did in the past. Your spouse's past is just that, their past, because it did not have anything to do with you. Unless something horrific happened in a past relationship that affects you, the past should never be mentioned because it is you who have the man.

Once I moved and had gotten my family settled in our new home, which was only about five miles away from our old one, I could now concentrate on the class reunion and prepare to go to Beaufort. From the list that I saw, I was expecting a pretty big showing. The board members planned a terrific weekend. We would meet at our old high school on Friday night, have a cookout and take a cruise in the Charleston harbor on Saturday night, and finally go to church service on Sunday. Finally, Terri decided that she would attend, but she was not coming to the entire function. She would come on Saturday and join me at the picnic. I was happy that she was coming, but the main reason she wanted to be there was because she wanted to show the people there that she indeed was a catch and if they even thought about rekindling any kind of relationship with me, it was not going to happen. I must admit, at 40 years old, she did not look a day over 25. She does not drink or smoke and she exercises regularly. At 5 feet 8 inches and 125 pounds, she was proud of the fact that she was the same size that she had been in high school.

Friday evening came and I picked up my cousin Ken, who graduated with me, and proceeded to Battery Creek High School for the class reunion. I had told several others who I saw and was amazed to know that they did not know anything about it. Of course, as I said before, they probably would not have come anyway because they were embarrassed with their progression in life. I was always told that the money you made should at least match your age. That means that if most of the people were 38 years old, they should have at least been making 38 thousand dollars annually. Many people in my hometown at that age were making a fraction of that, and it was even surprising to find out that in this day and age, a young person in their 30s could actually be on welfare. To me, welfare is something that you take as a last resort. I am sure the system has some value to those who really need it and are either fired, laid off, or are just incapable of working because of special circumstances, but it really sickens me to see a healthy person sit home all day long just to wait to receive a monthly check from the government. Amazingly enough, I even found out that some of the men were receiving unemployment checks and working under the table doing construction jobs and receiving cash. If you don't know what working under the table is, it is when you are working a regular job, but there are no checks and no taxes taken out. You are given cash for the work that you do.

You may be a criminal, illegally in the country, or just double dipping, but your boss will pay you cash for the amount of work that is performed. Double dipping is a term used when you collect a welfare check and still receive money under the table. When you do this, you are basically screwing the system and yourself. With nothing paid into social security, you won't get anything back. The guys I knew who were doing this didn't give a shit because they either did not expect to live that long to receive social security, or they thought that what the government paid for social security was chicken shit.

As my cousin Ken and I drove to the reunion, we were reminiscing about some of the girls that we expected to see and the ones who he had seen in the community. I was gone for so long, I did not have a clue of how some of my classmates looked. We walked in and greeted everyone there, but to my surprise, there was a total of about only 20 people. I was late and expected a crowd, but that was it. Though this reunion was set up beautifully, the participation was a disappointment.

Again, at least 100 people out of the graduating class were right there in town, and I am sure they knew about it because Tabitha, one of the main organizers, was still living there in town. She told me of all the people who had gotten the word, but just were not interested in coming. The women who were there did not look bad. I mean, a few of them had gained in excess of about 80 pounds, but besides being fat, they were successful and had good jobs. Ironically, as successful as some of the classmates were, there were only a couple of us who had gotten or still were married. Everyone who was there was doing something positive with his or her life.

Me and the other two guys who were there who had joined the Navy out of high school were all Chiefs. The others had jobs from mechanics, realty, and there was even a pastor. I thought that it was amazing that we were in high school together, went our separate ways, and then were able to find time in our busy lives to spend a weekend together. Though there were not a lot of people there, the first night was very good.

It was planned so very well, as our high school even had a football game that night. We took a group picture, had conversations, ate some food, and then found time to go to the field to cheer on the mighty dolphins of Battery Creek High.

After the game, my old friend Erick and I decided that we would go out for a few drinks, and some of the class members also wanted to join us. We ended up at a little hole in the wall a couple of miles away from the school. It was a new joint and many of the locals were there. Of course I was being told that I looked exceptionally well, but I had to put the compliment in its proper perspective. I do realize that I am not a bad-looking guy, but to them, I looked exceptionally well because I was being compared to the local guys. I still had all of my teeth in my head, they were white, and I was in decent shape. Also, when I spoke, the word jackass was not the first thing that came to mind. We left the bar and said our good-byes. We would meet the next day at the barbecue.

Sally called me at my mother's house that morning and asked me to meet her at the cookout before the rest of the classmates got there. She wanted me to cook the food, and I was a little apprehensive. She had done a marvelous job with the planning, and just a week earlier when her husband decided that he did not want to come, she asked me to drive the bus for the cruise we were having that night.

Now she was asking me to cook. I wanted to help as much as possible, but I also wanted to enjoy the event. I was starting to wonder if she thought I was Benson. I wanted to just wait for Terri to come and enjoy the cookout, not stand there cooking and smelling like smoke. I showed up early and got the fire started but I was relieved by a classmate who actually enjoyed cooking. Terri finally arrived when the cookout was almost over but she accomplished what she sought out to. She was two classes ahead of us in high school and she wanted to show everyone there how dynamic she still was. She did not say much, but she did not have to. A few more people showed up at the cookout who were not at the high school the first night. With them and their families, we had about 50 people there and had a very good time.

That night, we all met at a central place to go on the cruise. We were going to go to the Charleston harbor, and I was sure it was going to be a special night for all of us. I drove one van, and one of my friends drove the other. A couple more classmates had shown up to go on the cruise and we joked along the way as we were entering Charleston. Once there, we boarded the small boat for the short dinner cruise and listened to some great music by the band. It seemed so far away from the reality of the complex world, but when we all sat outside to chat, I then realized that many of them had real life issues that they were battling themselves. Everyone was laughing and having a good time, but when dinner was over and we really started to reminisce, they too had problems with teenage sons and daughters. They too were worried about the economy and the price of gas. They too were worried about retirement and social security. The getaway was wonderful but real life issues do not escape anyone for long. I found out that many people did not make the trip because of gas prices.

The price of gas had gone up to over four dollars a gallon in some cities like Atlanta, and a few classmates who lived there simply could not afford to come to the reunion. I never thought that I would see the day when the price of gas would play such a major role in making life decisions.

On our way back, I learned pretty much what everyone in the graduating class was doing and what they were not doing. As we made the 60-mile transit back to Beaufort, I started to reflect on my life and what I had achieved since I had been away. It made me realize that I was indeed lucky in many ways to not have indulged in drugs, and the discipline that I had received from the military had taken me a long way in life. I had learned how to think on my feet and be responsible for my actions. I had learned how to be tough, yet very compassionate. I had learned how to lead others in time of war and help mold lives during time of piece. I had learned how to hold my head up high during great times as well as times when adversity showed its evil head. I had learned that we should never judge a man by color or religion alone, but we must look at a man's heart and judge him or her based on their actions. I had learned that you won't always get respect, but you must always demand it. I had learned that all men are due respect regardless of their social status or annual salary. Most of all, I had learned to love myself and what I stood for. I realized that I truly did not have an enemy in world because all I ever tried to do was to give people respect and give back to those who had not been as fortunate as I was. I saw "Reflections" of all of my very young and unfortunate relatives who did not have a chance to make it as far as I had. I saw "Reflections" of Shone Kline, who I loved very much but was taken away much too soon. I saw "Reflections" of Collins Washington who use to work out with me daily. We would jog 3 miles in the hot summer heat, play 10 games of basketball, and jog back home, you left us too soon. I saw "Reflections" of Andrew Watson, who always had a smile on his face and not a mean bone in his body. I saw "Reflections" of Melanie Delaney, one of the sweetest young ladies that I have ever known, who left two children behind. I saw "Reflections" of Bruce Perry who died tragically, but will be remembered always. I saw "Reflections" of Cindy Houston, you were sweet and died much too young. Finally, I saw "Reflections" of my first cousin Christie Hazel, who was like a sister to me. I saw drugs tear apart one of the most beautiful women that I have ever known. These people left this world during the prime of their lives and for the most part, they all were special people.

Our short weekend was coming to an end, but in many ways, another chapter in my life was just getting started. To my mother, I love you because you always did the best you could. To my wife, I love you because you have always been the best mother that I have ever known. To my aunts, I love you all because you were just there. To my grandmothers and great grandmothers, you were always the backbone that made me whole. I have always heard that it takes a man to raise one. I tend to disagree because I know of a few great women who have raised law-abiding, respectable, and responsible men. Finally, to my father, we will probably never be what a father and son should be, but you taught me what a father shouldn't be. I will never blame you for anything because I feel that you were the best father that you knew how to be. You made me strong in many ways, and I now realize that I am not the victim—you are.

Printed in the United States
65048LVS00003B/424-438